SOUL STORIES

SOUL STORIES

Wisdom and Leadership Strategies for Flourishing African American Women

Foreword by
Rev. Dr. Nadine Burton

Editor
Rev. Dr. Charisse L. Gillett

chalice
PRESS

Cover concept by Teonicka Russell

Print: 9780827235731

EPUB: 9780827235748

EPDF: 9780827235755

ChalicePress.com

This book is dedicated

To those who mentored, cajoled, loved and challenged us to be all that God was calling us to be.

To the women whose stories are contained in this book and for those who see their stories in ours.

To those whose stories are yet to come.

To the women who through their lives, achievements, and aspirations made a path for others to follow.

In gratitude and with thanksgiving for your spirits.

Contents

Foreword
Rev. Dr. Nadine Burton ix

Preface and Acknowledgements
Rev. Dr. Charisse L. Gillett xi

A Life Made to Flourish: Cultivated by Unquenchable Joy
Rev. Dr. A. Denise Bell 1

A Table Prepared for Me: I Will Bring My Own Chair
Rev. Dr. LaTaunya M. Bynum 13

Growing into Ministry: Full Circle Moments
Rev. Dr. Nadine Burton 22

The Village is Undefeated: Surrounded by Faith
Rev. Dr. Dara Cobb-Lewis 32

An Ever-Flowing Stream: The Making of a River
Rev. Dr. Monique Crain Spells 43

Growing in the Margins: Searching for God
Rev. Joan Bell Haynes 50

I Am A Girl: I Stepped Out Because I Believed
Rev. Dr. Delesslyn A. Kennebrew 59

Leadership: Finding My Voice and My Way
Rev. Dr. Charisse L. Gillett 67

Vocational Leadership: The Convergence of Formation and Personal Transformation
Bishop Valerie Melvin 75

Where I Am From: Formed, Nurtured, and Shaped by Community
Rev. Terri Hord Owens *85*

Many Rivers to Cross: A Black Woman's Summation About Her Leadership, Spirituality and Community
Rev. Dr. Christal L. Williams *94*

An Encyclopedic Listing of African American Women Trailblazers: A Continuing Story in the Christian Church (Disciples of Christ)
Rev. Dr. Charisse L. Gillett *105*

Questions for Conversation and Reflection *123*

The African American Women Trailblazers *125*

Foreword

The African American Female Regional Ministers (AARMS) support group is rooted in Exodus 17:12-13. As Moses led God's people, his colleagues provided a stone for him to rest upon, and held his arms up, to lift the weight of ministry from his hands. While the other leaders held his hands up, the Israelites won the battles before them.

Our journey began in 2018, gathered around the table of The College of Regional Ministry. There were seven African American women who held regional judicatory roles in the Christian Church (Disciples of Christ) in the United States and Canada. We landed in regional ministry together and noticed each other. We began to see and hear each other, as our joys, celebrations, and challenges mirrored each other. We committed to holding each other's arms up, as we faced the daily battles and struggles of ministry. We committed ourselves to flourishing and celebrating our victories. To enable richer leadership development and deeper conversations, we applied for and received grant funding.

During this leadership development phase, we gathered in Hawaii in 2021 during Covid, to process our leadership experiences, and share, and then record our soul stories. One of the greatest blessings for me was to hear Bishop Valerie Melvin share, "from now on, just call me Hawaii!" because of the transformation that took place in her life. Hawaii transformed us and led us to hear our calls in new ways. Some of us moved into academia, others to general ministry, while some renewed their calls to regional work.

The same spiritual prodding that led us to create space for our care and flourishing, led us to water a seed planted by our Louisville Institute partners to write a book. This spiritual prodding also called us to affirm and invite other women leaders to the table. We are thankful to Rev. Terri Hord Owens, Rev. Dr. Delesslyn Kennebrew, and Rev. Dr. Monique Crain Spells for graciously accepting the invitation to share their story as part of this project.

We are filled with gratitude to be able to share our stories with you and the next generation of leaders. We move forward, flourishing in systems that keep us grounded in our faith and ever surrendering to the good work God began in us.

I am thankful for the support of the Black Leadership Project, Black Disciples Endowment Fund, Chalice Press, Christian Church Foundation, Disciples Home Missions, Lexington Theological Seminary, Louisville Institute, Mississippi Boulevard Christian Church, the Pension Fund, and last but certainly not least, the regions, colleagues, and family members who invested in our work as partners and mentors.

Rev. Dr. Nadine Burton

AARMS Convener

Preface and Acknowledgements

Friends,

Future generations will tell the story of seven African American female regional ministers in the Christian Church (Disciples of Christ) who sought to empower and encourage themselves by forming their own community of hope, and flourishing. The women came together as the African American Female Regional Ministers support group and met for more than a year in an intentional leadership development process. Their process of self-actualization and theological reflection is a powerful testament to their agency. It was my privilege to witness their strength, vulnerability, intellect, spirit, gifts for leadership, and capacity for growth.

On these pages you will encounter the lived experiences of these women and other African American women called into leadership. Their narratives are rooted in faith and family. Their narratives reflect upon those moments when others attempted to diminish their giftedness but only reinforced their call to serve a faithful God.

This book also bears witness to African American women trailblazers in the Christian Church (Disciples of Christ). These women broke barriers through their service on boards, committees and as leaders in positions of prominence in the Disciples church. Regretfully, not all women were identified, nonetheless, this encyclopedic listing is to be celebrated for those named.

I am grateful to Rev. Dr. Lawrence A. Q. Burnley, Ms. Ameila Webb Walker, Ms. May Reed, Ms. Marilyn F. Williams, and AARMS for researching and verifying information that helped to curate the final list. I am also grateful to Disciples Home Missions, the National Convocation, Disciples of Christ Historical Society, and the Office of the General Minister and President for institutional resources that contributed to the development of this list.

Rev. Tanya J. Tyler read drafts of this book and provided helpful suggestions to strengthen our narratives. Ms. Teonicka Russell's cover design beautifully reflects the flourishing spirit of each woman's journey. Thank you, Rev. Tyler and Ms. Russell, for your investment in this project. To Rev. Dr. Nadine

Burton, you held us together with your prayers and "no is not an option spirit." Thank you for your commitment to convening conversations that blessed our ministries and leadership as African American women.

In prose, poetry, and prayer these trailblazers tell us how they led, bloomed, thrived, and ultimately flourished. I invite you to read their soul stories.

With hope,

Rev. Dr. Charisse L. Gillett

Editor

A Life Made to Flourish
Cultivated by Unquenchable Joy

Rev. Dr. A. Denise Bell

Seeds of Joy

I was the third child of Richard and Bertha Bell, who moved from Charlottesville, Virginia, to Newark, New Jersey, in 1961, when I was three years old. My parents were part of the Great Migration from the South to the North, pursuing dreams of a better life. Along with my two older siblings—and later my younger brother, who was born in New Jersey—we were surrounded by a community of hardworking Southern transplants who did their best to protect and raise their children. Between working and raising us, my parents planted seeds of family and faith. We spent time with my grandmother, aunts, and uncles who had deep faith. Though our family wasn't a go-to-church-every-Sunday family, we attended enough to know that belief in God was non-negotiable. Those seeds of faith took root in my older brother and me, and we both became ordained clergy. Family and faith became our answers for every hard place.

My mother often shares the story of how, as an infant, I would wake up each morning giggling and smiling with joy to greet the day. Not much has changed over the many decades of my life. Joy has always been a key part of who I am, serving as fuel that has built endurance, resilience, and a love for God and others. I remember, as a child, the seed planted in my heart through a song I learned at Vacation Bible School: "I've got the joy, joy, joy, joy, down in my heart, down in my heart to stay."

That seed of joy took root and grew into my life's conviction that, "The joy of the Lord is my strength." My sense of joy was never silly, even though I've always had a gregarious laugh. My joy was about encouraging others, celebrating them, and fostering a collaboration of voices and actions to improve people's quality of life. I was a cheerleader, a team leader, and an exhorter. Over the years, cultivating joy and strength as a leader has been a hard-fought journey as a Black woman in ministry, personally and professionally. This essay is a conversation about a journey that inspired me to break through the challenges and obstacles of life to live and lead well with unapologetic joy and self-love.

Always being a deep thinker, I questioned everything—not to doubt, but to sort and to understand the meaning and the "so what" of life. I pondered everything I saw and heard. With eyes and ears opened wide, I'd watch and listen to my grandmother and aunts pray and hum until a smile would break forth on their faces from the inside out. That assured me, as a curious child, that everything was all right. Sunday school, Easter pageants, Christmas plays, Mother's Day, and Family and Friends Day were some of the things that stuck in my head to ponder: *Why all the fuss?* I thought there was a fuss every Sunday morning when the preacher preached himself into a frenzy—at least, that was my impression as a child. In reality, it was the crescendo of Black preaching, the celebration of a God who called us children, that made everything all right despite the ongoing fight for dreams, dignity, visibility, and equity in a society that rejected our humanity.

Rev. Dr. Martin Luther King Jr. and Mahalia Jackson mesmerized me. At the age of nine, I thought Dr. King was the king of Black people. I had never seen my mother cry; but, on the day of his death, I cried with and for my mother. My King was dead. When I heard Mahalia Jackson sing on TV, I felt like anything was possible. It was not as if I wanted to sing like her: I wanted to bring light, I wanted to bring joy! I did not fully understand or appreciate King's message or Jackson's deep spirituality expressed in song until we moved into an all-white community. While playing school with one of the neighborhood children, I said, "I want to be the teacher." The child replied, "You cannot be a teacher, you are a n****r. I was devastated. It was my mother's words that unclenched my fists and told me not to pay attention to the stupidity of others. Years later, my high school counselor told me college was not for me and that I should not bother with applications. Fortunately, I was a leader of Operation Push in New Jersey, a community action organization that advocated social justice, education, and youth empowerment. My first mentor, Rev. Dr. Buster Soaries, made it a requirement for all student leaders to go to college. Operation Push and Dr. Soaries shaped my character, values, and self-perception, which gave me enough fortitude not to be deterred by the stupidity of others.

In my college junior year, my father died. I was devastated. I was my father's daughter—I laughed like him, had dimples like him, and never met a stranger like him. When he died, I lost who I was. Before my father's death, my primary goal was to serve the wider community as a community activist. After my dad died, I realized that I needed an anchor, a more intrinsic motive that affirmed and celebrated life. Six months after my father's death, I heard my heart say: *I am lost and alone.* Staring at the bathroom mirror, eyesight blurred by salty tears, I remembered the stories of my youth. I asked God, "Are you the One that said You will never leave or forsake me?"

In that exact moment, I felt a warm, shower-like sensation from the top of my head to the bottom of my feet. The tears continued to flow. Instead of tears of grief alone, I cried tears of joy knowing that God loved me and would never leave or forsake me. I was no longer alone and have not been since that moment. The next day, I surrendered my life to Christ, and my journey toward flourishing began. I am an avid believer that true flourishing starts with a relationship with the Lord. Jesus reminds us that he is the vine, and we are the branches, and apart from him, we cannot grow and bear fruit (John 15:5). That day I became God's daughter! The house that I grew up in transformed into a place where the veil between heaven and earth becomes thin. The late Barbara Holmes says these are places where we "experience God unfiltered" (Holmes, 2022).

Two years after I gave my life to Christ, I had another experience. Holmes calls these "glimpses of the Holy in the context of our own lives, where the mystery of God unfolds and invites us to dance." I was attending a midweek service, sitting alone. I reflected on my life over the past two years, noticing that I was not the same person. I stopped hanging out with the wrong people and stopped feeling like I needed material things to make me feel good about myself. As I inquired of God about my life, I experienced a sensation of clarity: "You will proclaim the Gospel of Jesus Christ for the rest of your life." The church pew was another thin place.

Over the years, I have pondered this call as a helper in the transformation of others. I believe a key component of flourishing is personal clarity: What is your purpose? What is your passion? As Rev. Dr. Frank Thomas would often ask, "What do you believe about God?" Self-awareness and clarity are foundational to flourishing because they compel you to grow deeper, cultivate, and act.

That night at the church, I was confused but overjoyed. I was overjoyed because the Lord aligned my person with my purpose. Not long after, I enrolled at Denver Seminary in Denver, Colorado, to pursue a Master of Divinity degree. After being ordained and over the course of thirty-six years, I have served the church in various roles: Navy chaplain candidate, pastor, associate pastor, senior associate, campus pastor, executive pastor, interim pastor, operations pastor, and regional minister. I traveled across the country to create healthy and vital spaces so that the Gospel of Jesus Christ could be expanded. One "yes" led to another, and before I knew it, I had finished my PhD program. This led me to my most important job: the honor of teaching pastoral leadership at Lexington Theological Seminary.

A More Excellent Way

As I look back over my life, I often wonder how I got from one place to the next. Leadership is built from one small thing after another. Every time a door opened, I stepped through it. I'm reminded of unsolicited opportunities to lead or participate in significant actions to help groups or organizations arrive at solutions that served everyone. I was the person who knew how to affirm and ask questions to explore "a more excellent way." As a result, I received opportunities to try new things and chart new paths. I realized even as a young adult that I could listen and ask meaningful questions—not to threaten the leader in the room but to invite everyone to think about the best outcome.

For instance, I belonged to a high school sorority where a heated discussion about membership requirements took place; despite intense fear, I stood up and raised my hand. When the room became quiet, I suggested an option that confirmed we all wanted the same thing. To reiterate my point, I emphasized that everyone had a right to their opinion, and as a service organization of young women, we had choices. I understood those choices from the voices in the room. My peers appreciated how I helped facilitate a way forward; and, at the next election, I was named vice president for two years. Unlike the usual officers who were bold, mature-looking seniors, I was quiet, of small stature, and a junior in high school. I felt the pressure to push past my fear to navigate both internal and external negative voices. Having no other choice but to lean into my team leader/exhorter persona, I became a clarifying and collaborative voice in the room. I am still that clarifying and collaborative voice. I have always trusted the Lord to guide my steps and have always felt I was serving where I needed to be. Before each ministry assignment, I would ask God, "Am I doing what you sent me here to do?" While I never had to actively search for church positions, or any job for that matter, each role has required significant personal sacrifices due to challenging organizational structures. These challenges typically fell into three categories.

First, hierarchical systems were in place to monitor, measure, and control my every movement to ensure I was fulfilling my paid duties. Second, discriminatory practices rooted in chauvinism, sexism, racism, and marriage bias functioned to limit my advancement and "keep me in my place." Third, I served in church cultures that expected a loving pastor to perform all duties and responsibilities while remaining available around the clock. As an unmarried female pastor, I was especially vulnerable to these unrealistic expectations, making it impossible to maintain healthy boundaries between my personal and professional life.

Structures can be difficult to identify because such constructs are often embedded in innocent assumptions that surface in everyday conversations. People would ask questions like:

> "What part of Africa are you from?"
> "Where is your husband?"
> "Isn't that your job?"
> "Why don't you have time?"
> "You don't have any kids?"
> "Are you a lesbian?"

These questions revealed underlying biases about race, marital status, professional responsibilities, and availability that shaped how others viewed my role and capacity as a pastor. I was on a constant quest not to let my internal judgments about myself morph into the biased judgments of uninformed organizational structures.

I recall a time in my life when I was entangled by these biases, when I felt robbed of choice and personal agency. The church I was serving was experiencing difficult circumstances. I noticed that whenever I returned after taking a period of rest, something worse happened. So I stopped resting and morphed into the strong Black woman, problem solver, and chief caregiver. I reasoned that if I loved the church and wanted to be effective, I did not have a choice. As a result, I became mentally, physically, and spiritually exhausted. It didn't cause me to question my call at the time, but it made me rethink how I was doing ministry and how I saw myself in the role. I was yearning to be more than just a role.

I sought support and joined a Pastoral Excellence program funded by Lilly Endowment Inc. (LEI). The first session was Ministry 101, and I learned right away that ministry is not the entirety of life. The program emphasized peer support, self-care, and scholarship. The group included fifteen people, mostly men. While our stories about the high demands of ministry were similar, the biases we faced in our ministries varied. My male colleagues were all married with supportive wives, which usually meant someone else took care of the cooking, laundry, and cleaning without additional cost. As a single woman in a demanding ministry role, I had to pay for home care services to keep my home well-maintained. This financial burden often made me feel isolated as I balanced both my ministry responsibilities and the demands of managing a household alone.

The disparity in our experiences highlighted not only the barriers faced by women in ministry but also the underlying societal expectations that often remain unchallenged. Societal expectations are real and vary by gender, but I realized they did not have to shape my expectations for myself. I stepped back, prioritized my home life and self-care, and enrolled in a PhD program. I learned from this experience that if unchecked, we can resent the insensitivity, demands, and expectations imposed upon us by the institutions we serve. However, the bottom line is that no one will love me more than I love myself—or even more than the Lord!

"Loving me best" means that no matter how much I care about my church, family, friends, and coworkers, they are not responsible for advising me on how to handle life's challenges. They also cannot demand that I do what's best for me through their eyes. I am responsible for my own well-being. Therefore, I must do my work to flourish and become my best self. That is my job. With the support and help of others, I have found a more excellent way.

Persist, Pivot but Never Give Up

It was an exciting and difficult experience to finish the PhD program. It took me twelve years to complete. The first three and a half years were coursework. The rest of the time was fraught with starts and stops, do-overs, and rewrites. There were many midnight hours when I wanted to quit, but the Lord would not let me. Even when I was in the middle of writing my last comprehensive exam (there were four), despite how far I had come, I was convinced I was going to fail. I still had the voice of that high school counselor in my head, *Don't bother; you are not smart enough.*

It was ten o'clock in the morning. I had been working eight days straight with very little sleep. I was crying with crocodile tears, asking the Lord to show me how to quit. Suddenly, out of nowhere, the song "Never Give Up" by Yolanda Adams filled the room:

Visions that can change the world, trapped inside an ordinary girl.
She looks just like me, too afraid to dream out loud.
And though it's set for your idea, it won't make sense to everybody.

You need courage now, if you're going to persevere,
To fulfill your divine purpose, you've gotta answer when you're called,
So don't be afraid to face the world against all odds.
Keep the dream alive; don't let it die
If something deep inside keeps inspiring you to try, don't stop
Never give up; don't ever give up on you. Don't give up (Adams, 2001).

To this day, I do not know where the music came from. I needed courage and fortitude, and the Lord provided. So, I dried my eyes, got off the floor, pulled from a place deep inside, and finished. It was another encounter with the Lord—another thin place. I passed all four of my comprehensive exams and later received the "Dissertation of the Year" award. What would have happened if I had quit? *Whatever you do, don't quit!* That became my mantra for life.

After completing the coursework in my PhD program, I was faced with what seemed like a mountain that I could never climb—the dissertation process. In the first few years, I thought I had to climb it alone. The message that I received as a Black woman in the dissertation process was that "this is an independent process." I was not properly informed that "independent" did not mean "in isolation." There were many lonely nights and tearful days before I finally realized that I needed to turn to my family and friends. First, I needed to tell the truth—that I was not alright. Secondly, I needed to invite them in to laugh, cry, pray, and counsel with me. Vulnerability was a different kind of place. Because I spent so much time fighting to prove I was qualified for the places my call led me, I kept vulnerability at arm's length. Yet, embracing vulnerability helped me relax in my strength, acknowledge my limitations, and learn to rest properly.

During my program, I wrestled with myself and the organizations I served. I felt guilty. I would imagine an unfaithful spouse feeling torn at the heart. While studying, I felt like I needed to work; while at work, I felt like I needed to study. I had four job changes that elevated my career and deepened my experience in executive church leadership. Today, I would advise against doing this—it's best to remain in one place until you complete your program, if possible. However, for this Black woman with dreams, it was impossible to say "no" to opportunities when they presented themselves. This period was challenging because not every organization I worked with cared about my academic success. When I requested leniency, the response was, "You still have to do your job." I had the impression that my male coworkers who also pursued terminal degrees received more leeway.

Gender issues regarding education were a reality long before my PhD program. I remember being in seminary as the only African American female student with feeling that I was there by fluke. I had to remind professors that the traditions of White Western Christianity were not the tenets of Christianity; thus, those traditions are not the standards to be used to judge the Black church. Cautiously aware of being the only Black woman, I refused to allow them to describe the Black church as deficient. Not only did I tussle with faculty but also with fellow students. More times than I can remember, someone mistakenly took me as somebody's wife, there to bring my husband dinner while he studied at the library. On one occasion, a man suggested I had an independent spirit and needed prayer. This was the last straw for me and the Lord. My faith and trust in God's call in my life spoke back to me. That moment made me realize that convincing others where I should be ministry-wise was not my fight. That was God's job.

Navigating unchallenged societal expectations surfaced often in my ministry. I recall a time when I served as executive pastor under the expectation that I was to do as I was told. In this context, an attitude perpetuated by the perception of clergy as employees and my status as a single woman permitted those whom I served to disrespect me. Nothing in my leadership handbook said that I was a puppet. The assignment had become uncomfortable. Eventually, lay leadership could not see a healthy partnership between clergy and laity. I listened to their complaint, did not argue its validity, and asked, "Do you want to fire me?"

Such a question could have been dangerous—they could have said yes. I needed to understand their ultimate intentions, and I needed them to realize that I was not afraid. I remained calm and composed, hoping to help them understand that addressing this issue could improve our church practices, even if it came at my own expense. I trusted that the Lord would protect me. It was a teaching moment—if not for them, then for me.

Teaching moments became a tool that taught me how to respond rather than react to challenging leadership situations. As an executive leader, I encountered churches where leadership was not positional but situational, and out of convenience, there always seemed to be a script where I was to acquiesce to others in the room. Sometimes it was indirect, and other times it was obvious. It was not always easy for me to determine if it was because I was Black or if it was because I was a woman. It was a lot of mental work. After a few years of walking the tightrope, I've had enough. I leaned deeper into my spiritual disciplines. This brought me closer to God and served as the foundation for a new script of godly discernment. I had discovered a place where my clarifying and collaborative voice could make a difference. It worked every time! I invited the presence of God in such a way that joy became a leading factor in everything that I did. Even if I lost track of joy-filled and life-giving practices, I could always find my way back. Like reading a good book, it's easy to pick up right where you left off.

In situations where ministry assignments became uncomfortable, I learned to pivot to discover a more excellent way. I learned the importance of being self-aware, improving relationships, cultivating connections and networks, mentoring and peer relationships, and practicing self-care and personal development. Yes, sometimes engaging in therapeutic relationships and spiritual direction made a difference. No matter how powerful the call is or how profound the purpose, we cannot do it alone. Jesus modeled the importance of companionship and partnership by calling the twelve disciples and others to accompany him in revealing God's redemptive plan for humanity. It took me a moment to realize how vital companionship was on the journey.

One key insight during my ministry was learning not to take things personally. People react based on the angle of their worldview. I cannot position myself at their angle, but I can acknowledge their angle, help them articulate it, and realize that it has nothing to do with me. Repair and restoration are God's job. I have always believed in the power of honoring everyone's the personhood. According to Rev. Terri Hord Owens, the General Minister and President of the Christian Church (Disciples of Christ), it is about, "keeping people clothed in their dignity." One of my values is to assist individuals in preserving their dignity and their longing to be integrated into their faith communities of choice. Although not always easy, by staying self-aware and not taking things as a personal affront, I have realized that it is not about me. I had to confide in many friends, peers, mentors, and a therapist along the way to make sure it wasn't me. And when it was me, I had to do work to address my issues and be transparent in the community.

No matter what, the church as an organization is part of God's creation. Churches are messy, naturally resistant to change. They are a crucible of power dynamics, yet they ultimately remain a steward of God's mission to the world. I found it a privilege to help ignite the passion and gifts of people, so that they can go out to impact and change the world. Indeed, the human structures that make up the church are beautiful and broken vessels that span the spectrum of human experience. Being a servant leader and shepherd over the lives of individuals and congregations has been a privilege, and I have had incredible experiences within the church. Navigating the highs and lows of leadership across the church created some crucible moments that shaped me into a person who walks with authority. Rev. Dr. Frank Thomas taught me the value of asserting one's authority in a way that I will always remember. The liberation that emerged from the crucible experiences has positioned me to where I no longer need permission from people, structures, or hierarchies to tell me that I have value, worth, or self-agency to be or do whatever God has called me to be and do.

As the Donald and Lillian Nunnelly Endowed Chair of Pastoral Leadership at LTS, I want to thank the girl from my childhood neighborhood who told me, "You're a n…gg…. You can't be a teacher." Thank you. This terminal degree and Dissertation of the Year Award are my way of saying "thank you" to the high school guidance counselor who told me not to apply to college. My almost 40 years of service to Christ's church are in response to that man who said I was too independent and in need of prayer. I am a part of a fantastic seminary whose mission is to educate students to be faithful leaders who will strengthen the church around the world. I want to say this to the church leaders I worked with who were resistant to my leadership: Thank you.

Greek poet Dinos Christianopoulos once said, "They tried to bury us, but they didn't know we were seeds." (Christianopoulos, 1995). This quote always makes me think about the obstacles and challenges I've faced. They tried to put me in my place, as if they were attempting to bury my potential, calling, and dreams. My status as a seed went unnoticed. I am a seed that will continue to grow into a harvest of joy, love, and service. If you're familiar with the process, you might recall that seeds, once planted in the dark earth, develop into both a shoot and a root and eventually produce good fruit.

Our purpose in life is to flourish as we grow and evolve in fulfilling our calling to serve and transform the lives of others.

Wisdom For the Next Generation

- Create spaces in your life to affirm who you are—your relationship with God, your sense of calling, your gifts, passions, aspirations, and your path of preparation. Some people schedule regular annual retreats or regularly journal about life.
- Flourishing invites family and supportive friends to journey with you to help you stay on track.
- Obstacles and challenges are a part of the journey that cannot be avoided. They should be expected. So prepare for them. Reach out

to persons who can mentor you in navigating rough terrain as a leader. Reach out to another sister who can glean from your wisdom.

- Create a record of the thin places in your life where your encounter with the Holy changed the trajectory of your life.
- Don't take it personally; stand strong! Jesus taught the disciples that structures of power will rise against them because of who they represent (John 15:18-25, NIV). Your very presence as a leader challenges systems that were designed to relegate you to a lower status. Resistance builds resilience!
- Develop life-giving, joyful, and spiritual practices that draw you closer to God, yourself, and others.

A Final Word

My story is about discovering a path toward flourishing. It's about finding the joy that becomes strength in the midst of institutional bias, personal loss, and professional challenges. It's about learning that you are responsible for your own well-being; that community is essential but must be by invitation rather than demand; and that not everything is about you—even when it feels personal.

If you are someone who has been told that you're not enough, not smart enough, not the right fit—this story is for you. If you're navigating spaces where you're the only one and feeling the weight of representation—this story is for you. If you're trying to lead with integrity while others expect you to diminish yourself—this story is for you.

The path to flourishing requires the courage to step through doors when they open, the wisdom to know when to say no, and the spiritual maturity to distinguish between what is yours to carry and what belongs to God. It means learning to love yourself well enough to maintain boundaries, finding your clarifying voice in the room, and trusting that your purpose is bigger than others' limited perceptions.

Most importantly, it's about discovering that the joy you carry—through tears and opposition—can become an unshakeable foundation. When you know who you are and whose you are, when you surround yourself with genuine community, and when you remain open to those thin places where God meets you, you don't just survive—you flourish.

Your journey may look different, but the invitation is the same: to live fully, lead authentically, and trust that you, too, were made to flourish.

— ***Rev. Dr. A. Denise Bell*** *is the Donald and Lillian Nunnelly Endowed Chair for Pastoral Leadership at Lexington Theological Seminary.*

References

Adams, Y. (2001). "Never Give Up" [Song] on *Believe* [Album]. Elektra Records

Barbara Holmes. (2022, November 18). Experiencing God in the Thin Places with Barbara Holmes, *CONSPIRE 2021 (Day One)*, [Video]. YouTube. https://www.youtube.com/watch?v=fVkXNjj7YNI.

Christianopoulos, D. (1995). *The body and the wormwood* (N. Kostis, Trans.). Odysseas. (Original work published 1960-1993)

A Table Prepared for Me

I Will Bring My Own Chair

Rev. Dr. LaTaunya M. Bynum

Jesus loves me, this I know,
for the Bible tells me so.
Little ones to him belong.
They are weak, but he is strong.

I am a church girl. My parents took me and my siblings to church from before the time I had any memory. I did my first public speaking in church—first in simple four-line Easter and Christmas speeches as a child and later as a teenager on Youth Sunday. My mother was a second-generation member of the Christian Church (Disciples of Christ); my father was a lifelong Missionary Baptist. We lived close enough to United Christian Church in Los Angeles for my parents to get us dressed and fed on Sunday morning and then drive us to Sunday School. Afterwards, we would go home, get dressed, and bring my mother to church in time for her to get robed and take her place in the choir. Then my father would drive to Metropolitan Baptist Church, a few miles from United, where he would take his place among the deacons.

The people in my home church modeled Christian living for me. They were caring, loving, and they taught us to love God and to be compassionate. They taught us manners, respect, and what it means to be part of a faith community. They encouraged us, assuring us that if we trusted in God, got a good education, and worked hard to achieve our goals, we could do anything we set out to do.

The lessons I learned growing up at United Christian Church helped me cope with my first experience of racism. It happened on the first day of church camp at Loch Leven in the Pacific Southwest Region of the DOC. We were lined up for something and there was a White boy in front of me. At some point the boy turned around, looked at me and said, "You Negro." His tone of voice suggested that, for him, Negro was a pejorative term and I was not a person he needed to value. Somewhere, an eight-year-old White kid had learned that being an eight-year-old Black kid was a bad thing. I noted what he said, and how it was said. His words told me he believed in his eight-year-old superiority to me and people who looked like me. I did not have the language then, but now I know he had already been influenced by White supremacist culture.

The experience of being othered did not make me angry at that moment, though I have clearly not forgotten it. I suppose it was because there were adults there and elsewhere that I trusted and who helped me feel safe. In Sunday School, in choir, in my household and extended family, I was surrounded by people who let me know that being othered by someone really had little to do with who I was or who I would become. My parents understood that race and the fact that my sister and I were girls would be limiting to some people, but they encouraged us not to let it be a barrier to ourselves. I have never forgotten that lesson, and so I assume that there are no tables in the church at which I am not welcome to take a seat.

They'll Know We Are Christians by Our Love

When I was fourteen, I returned to Loch Leven for Christian Youth Fellowship camp and to learn to sing and live "They will know we are Christians by our Love" and "Pass it On." I learned to live Micah 6:8 and Matthew 7:12 NIV. Micah 6:8 reads He has shown you, O mortal, what is good. And what does the Lord require of you? To act justly and to love mercy and to walk humbly with your God. Matthew 7:12 NIV read So, in everything, do to others what you would have them do to you, for this sums up the Law and the Prophets. I was surrounded by caring adults and youth leaders, mostly young White men, who helped broaden my understanding of ministry and the church. They were the antidote to my first camp experience. They, along with my home church, helped me make the connection between faith and social justice.

It was during that second camp experience that I discerned that I was a person whose voice could speak a word of hope and justice, someone who could speak truth to power, someone who could listen in the discomfort of truth being spoken to me and others. I was discerning the power of God in the room and how God's power allowed me to impact situations for the better. I know I have the gift of giving verbal cues. I can use a phrase or say a word that will get picked up by people in the room. I learned that my voice and the words I speak are powerful tools for me to use with wisdom and an awareness of what needs to be said and done.

It was also during that week at camp that I discerned a call to ministry. I shared with my pastor, Enoch Henry, that I was feeling a call to what we then called full-time Christian service. He called forward me and a boy who had also been at camp that week and who had also made the same decision; and he asked us to share our call stories with the congregation. It was a bold statement for a shy, skinny kid like me to make, but I did.

After I publicly announced my call to ministry, I began to understand the truth of what my parents meant when they told my sister and me that people would make limiting statements based on our gender. I began to learn how sexism and misogyny operate to gaslight and undermine women's dreams, and how women can participate in perpetuating patriarchal ideas about women's roles.

The announcement of my call was greeted mainly with positive affirmations. But there was one woman in the church, a retired teacher, who told me I could be a missionary overseas or a pastor's wife, but I could not be the minister or pastor. Here is where I have to say that I cannot abide bullies, and what she said was bullying at its best. Being told by someone how God spoke to me seemed to be nonsense to me. The call had come to me, and I would respond to it as I was led, and so I did.

From that camp and call experience, I met one of my mentors and leaders. He was a young White pastor named Dennis, now of blessed memory, who in the late 1960s served for a year as the associate pastor of my home church. He, along with others, helped me see that being committed to peace and justice is an act of faith and that ministry can be hard, fun, and joyful—sometimes all at the same time. These mentors helped me learn to take my ministry seriously, but not myself so seriously that I cannot laugh and enjoy life.

I remembered those lessons while I studied at Chapman College and at the School of Theology at Claremont. When I entered Claremont in 1976, their basic terminal degree was the Doctor of Ministry, and that was the program I entered. One of the first elective classes I took was a course on liberation theology. I was introduced to the writings of James Cone (*Black Theology and Black Power*; *God of the Oppressed*), Rosemary Radford Ruether (*Liberation Theology*) and Paulo Freire (*Pedagogy of the Oppressed*). My Doctor of Ministry project was a preview of what would become womanist theology, "Black and Feminist Theology: A New Word About God" (1980). As I studied and developed friendships—a few of which continue to this day—I imagined what my ministry might look like. It did not include congregational ministry. There were too few places for women, especially women of color, at the time.

I imagined chaplaincy or some kind of social justice ministry. But I had not imagined how long it would take to find a full-time call.

Spirit of God, Descend Upon my Heart...Teach Me the Patience of Unanswered Prayer

I did everything I was supposed to do to graduate from high school, go to college, and graduate in four years. I did everything I was supposed to do to go to seminary and get a degree (D.Min and M.Div., which Claremont added in 1978). I did everything I was supposed to do to get ordained and answer a call to a specific ministry. But that did not happen according to the expected time frame. That last year of seminary was a year of recovery, where I took time off. My father, Charley Bynum Jr. died a few weeks before I began my final year in seminary. He was a protector for our family and a champion for my sister and me. It was a sudden and unexpected passing that left our family shaken, but we persevered.

Pass Me Not, O Gentle Savior

In those months after graduation and ordination, I attended several clergy groups. While I was in the room, mostly male Black ministers affirmed my gifts and qualifications; likewise, mostly male White ministers did the same. However, more than one minister at different meetings would say something along the lines of, "I would call you to serve in my church if I could, but I don't know how the women would react to a woman minister." I am not convinced that resistance came only from women in the church. Saying that was a way to deflect their own fear and resistance to women in ministerial leadership.

I did secular work for a year and a half after graduation and ordination and occasionally preached. But I felt rejected by the church I had loved and not valued by people who said they respected my gifts. I do not doubt that if I was embodied as a White heterosexual man, I would not have waited so long for a call to settled ministry.

Eventually I was asked to serve as the interim pastor of a small, dying congregation in Lynwood, California, which was formerly nearly all-White but now mostly African American. It averaged six to ten people per Sunday. It was where I learned to prepare a sermon every week. It was where I presided over my first funerals. It was where I learned the rhythms of pastoral and congregational life. I wondered what the next thing to happen in my ministry.

The next thing came in the form of an invitation to apply for a Clinical Pastoral Education program (CPE) at Saint Elizabeth's Hospital, which at the time was a sprawling mental hospital in Washington, D.C. After being accepted into the 12-month program, I was assigned to work on the forensics unit, where people who were guilty of crimes but deemed too mentally ill for prison were housed. The classes we took when we were not on our wards helped me gain some understanding about group dynamics and leadership. I also learned that if I can, I will challenge leadership when I believe it to be unjust.

My CPE experience was so meaningful to me that I began to imagine a ministry of chaplaincy. I began thinking about what it would take for me to become a CPE supervisor. But then came the phone call that defined the trajectory of my ministry.

During a weekly meeting with my CPE supervisor, an ordained Southern Baptist woman, I was venting my frustration at not having received a call. She asked me a pivotal question, "What would you do if you got the call to the ministry you really want?" My response was that I had committed to being at Saint Elizabeth's for 12 months, and since I only been there for six, I would choose to complete the program. She asked me to think some more about what I had just said and to be open to how the Spirit could move in my life and ministry.

In those days, there were no cell phones, faxes, or internet. Pink paper pads were used to record telephone messages. When I came out of my supervisor's office, there was a message for me from the executive secretary of the Department of Ministry in the Division of Homeland Ministry (DHM), requesting a call back. I called, and the executive secretary wanted to know if I would be interested in being considered for the position of Director of Women in Ministry. I was interested but hesitant. I had a stack of rejection letters telling me that although I was gifted, I was not quite right for the ministry position for which I had applied.

Still, I flew out to Indianapolis for interviews and was called to the position. I served in that position for twelve years. For several months I also worked for the Department of Church Women. Through all those years, my call was to support and advocate for all women who had not gained the respect for their leadership and their contributions to the church that they deserved. It was rewarding work that introduced me to many people and places around the United States and Canada. I believe I helped seed the ground for the progress of women in the church throughout my ministry. I remain committed to the sacred work of seeing and encouraging the church to see and receive the gifts of women in leadership.

My time ended at DHM during one of its transitional periods. There were meetings and conferences on what DHM should look like and how it should be structured. By this time, the President of DHM and the Vice President of the Center for Leadership and Development (formerly, the Department of Ministry CLD was a combination of several departments) were both women.

I remember saying in one staff meeting that whatever staffing decisions were going to be made should not be made by the committee. The president did not need a new team of vice presidents. She and the existing vice presidents should make the hard decisions. The day came when the president's secretary called to say the president wanted to see me after lunch. I walked down to her office, and when I got there, she started to cry. I sensed what was coming. I decided to let her speak rather than rescue her by asking if I was being fired. She began, "You're one of the best staff members I've got. But…"

My job was being cut—and so was I. Stunned and disappointed, I walked back to my office. On the way, I passed the open door of one of the vice presidents. She asked if we needed to talk. I said we did, but not today. I headed home. Being let go devastated me, because I knew the value I brought through advocating for women in ministry. I felt betrayed and disrespected both personally and professionally.

Eventually, I recovered. Recovery was not a quick or easy process. It required letting myself feel my anger and disappointment, and those feelings called me to prayer, reflection, and forgiveness. Over the years and after a lot of hard conversations, I am on good terms as colleagues and friends with both the women who made the decision to eliminate my position.

In Times Like These

I believe God has always prepared me for the next ministry, even when I did not know where that place would be. I regained my love of ministry and learned to be a pastor during a nine-month interim ministry at an all-White Bethany Christian Church in Lincoln, Nebraska. I officiated a few weddings and presided over several funerals. I learned the importance of sitting at the bedside of someone in the hospital and sharing a cup of coffee and a snack in someone's home. The congregation was accepting, kind, and helpful to me during those months.

While serving at Bethany, I was also in Search and Call, a network for ministers seeking employment in a congregation or church-related organization. I had a range of experiences since ordination and being at that Nebraska congregation prepared me for the call to serve as the pastor of Broad Street Christian Church in Columbus, Ohio.

When I went there, it was a stable interracial, welcoming congregation a few miles from downtown Columbus. I served there for eleven years. I learned to deal with what I call the "Faust Effect," named in memory of Floyd Faust who came to the congregation as a young man in 1929 and who retired in 1973. I arrived in 1996 when he was still part of the living memory of most of the members. He was kind and mostly let me do ministry in my own way, but I did have to overcome a lot of things that began with, "Dr. Faust never did it that way" and "Dr. Faust always did it that way."

During my time at Broad Street, I served on the board of the National Convocation and was its vice president when the practice was that the vice president was in line to be the next president. But that did not happen with me. I made a mental note of the practice not being followed but did not say anything publicly.

I also served the General Board and several other General Church committees. My favorite was the Committee for Renewal and Structure. That committee recommended to the General Assembly changes in our Design and any approvals for regional or general church realignment.

The highlight of my service to the General Board was being asked to chair the search committee for the person who would be called and elected so serve as General Minister and President (GMP) of the Christian Church (Disciples of Christ) in the United States and Canada. That person would be approved at the General Assembly in Portland in 2005. The search committee's choice was an African American woman named Lois Artis, who was serving as the president of the Church Finance Council. She was well qualified to serve as the Disciples' GMP. The committee was stunned and disappointed that the Executive Committee of the General Board declined to forward her name to the General Board and then to the General Assembly.

Despite the disappointment and anger, each of us on the search committee agreed to begin again. Through the process of collecting ministerial profiles, a candidate emerged. What happened after the unsuccessful nomination of Lois Artis felt like an affirmation of my ministry advocating for women. We were able to nominate and celebrate the call and election of Sharon E. Watkins to be the Disciples' first woman GMP. And what a joy it was to know that Sharon was succeeded by Terri Hord Owens, the first African American woman to serve as head of communion in a mainline church.

Yet at Broad Street, we had begun to see the results of church decline—lower attendance, no growth, declining offerings. The decline exposed issues in the church. I was on sabbatical in the spring of 2005, returning just before the General Assembly in Portland, Oregon, where Sharon would be elected. One of our elders wanted to know why I would be gone several days to General Assembly when I had just returned from sabbatical. I reminded her that it was my responsibility to shepherd the GMP vote. She said I should have flown from Columbus to Portland for the vote and then come right back.

There were other issues; but what mattered was that, while I had solid support in the congregation, I eventually lost the support of the board and the elders. Another mentor from my church camp days who was serving a large church in Columbus invited me to lunch. He asked me if I had done all that I was called to do in the congregation. It took more than a year for me to get to where I could confidently say, "yes, I have done all that can do here." When I reached that point, I was able to move on from the congregation. In 2007, I joined the regional staff of the Christian Church in Ohio.

That's When You Blessed Me

I served on the regional staff for seven years staffing the anti-racism training process; working with Ohio Disciples Women; staffing Advance Ministries, a ministry for young adults; and representing the region in five districts. It was a fulfilling ministry, and I was privileged to work with and become friends with people I continue to consider colleagues.

Over time, fissures began to appear in Ohio—a lack of trust among some clergy of regional leadership; an entrenched sense that Ohio was a region that could stand on its own without support or help from the General Church; resistance to change; and declining membership and finances. When it became clear that staff cuts would need to be made, people began lamenting with me that I needed to seek ministry elsewhere; the assumption was, from my perspective, that I would be the one to leave.

I had already entered Search and Call because there was a region in search of a regional minister, and I wanted to be considered. I knew that Northern California-Nevada was the right fit for me because when I mentioned having a same-gender partner, no one on the committee reacted negatively. (She is now my wife). When I was asked if I would accept the call if it were offered, I said yes. The call was extended, and I am now in my 11th year as Regional Minister. This region is not without all the challenges other regions experience—how to help small-membership congregations thrive, too few finances, and people stretched thin by their love for the church. This ministry has given me space to use my voice to speak words of leadership, justice, challenge, and hope, and it has been good.

Wisdom for The Next Generation

I want to encourage young women and women new to ministry to:

- Stay at the table. When necessary, bring a chair if one is not provided for you.
- Let your voice be one that advocates for diversity, equity, and inclusion.
- We are in a church that identifies itself as a "movement for wholeness in a fragmented world." Do what you can to bring honest reconciliation and wholeness to the places where there is fragmentation, and always, always, always own your part in brokenness you helped cause.
- Trust that God has prepared you for the tables you will pull up to and that God is trustworthy and able to provide you with what you need to take your seat.
- Pray hard, work hard, and find a supportive community who will laugh and cry with you.
- Have fun. This is God's doing, and God wishes us joy.

A Final Word

This is my last call. I will retire in 2026, and I am sure God is already preparing me for the next thing. There is a collection of stories of Black women ordained in the 1970s and 1980s I want to curate. There are issues I want to speak to in opposition to these authoritarian times, and I want to mentor as much as I can a generation or two of women ministers and their colleagues. Years ago, before I was ordained, I complained to a regional minister about being a token member of a committee. He said to me, "That may be true, but you are on the committee, you have the agenda, and you are sitting at the table. *They* may think of you as a token. You don't have to think of yourself that way."

What has kept me at these various tables is my understanding that I am where I need to be because God has called me to be there. So, I *Believe I'll Run On, See What the End Is Gonna Be.*

— ***Rev. Dr. LaTaunya M. Bynum*** *is the Regional Minister of the Christian Church (Disciples of Christ) in Northern California-Nevada.*

Growing Into Ministry

Full Circle Moments

Rev. Dr. Nadine Burton

My Stones

In chapter one of the Book of Joshua, the Israelites crossed the Jordan River into their promised land. As they crossed the river, they laid down twelve stones that represented the twelve tribes of Israel. Each time God showed up in their lives, each time there was a victory, or each time they became aware of the presence of God, a stone was laid, representing an altar of remembrance. As a Christian leader and African American woman, the stones in my life are laid open before you in this narrative. They revolve around my spiritual formation, my call and pastoral identity, and coming to love God—who loves me unconditionally, the one who continues to teach me to love myself and the people of God.

I grew up in a two-parent, loving home in Memphis, Tennessee. My parents were Maurice and Lillie B. Burton. We were ten siblings and two parents living in a four-room house on Eyers Road. I was reared in a Christian home. My parents loved God, and they taught us to love God. My father was a deacon and superintendent of the Sunday School. My mother was a member of the diaconate and a volunteer with the women's auxiliaries. We grew up poor; however, we did not know we were poor. Our parents always provided for us. My mother could take flour and potatoes and make them stretch for days. On Sundays after church, there was always enough food. Neighbors would come over for a piece of my mom's pound cake, meatloaf, and spaghetti. My daddy raised chickens, hogs, cows, and pigs and slaughtered them for winter meat. I learned the gravity of my daddy's hustle to feed us at his funeral, hearing friends speak about his character and integrity.

My parents made each one of us feel that we were the favorite child. We had to choose whether we would go to college, find a job, or enter the armed services. For those bound for college, there were no scholarships or college funds, only government Pell grants and student loans. We lost our father in May 2004 and our mother in August 2008. Today, my siblings are close. I thank God for the love my siblings showed me, for the ways they protected and sacrificed for me while growing up and for the love that we have for God and each other today.

When I was in the sixth grade, my teacher, Mr. Branch, asked me to be the classroom monitor while he stepped into the hallway for an emergency talk with another teacher, Ms. Stidum. He told me to record the names of the students who misbehaved by writing them on the bulletin board. I knew stepping into this role would bring ridicule, but Mr. Branch sought me out. I said yes to this assignment. When he left, the students immediately began to cut up. I remember two male students specifically. I started writing names on the board. The students taunted and teased me for following the rules. Insulting and nasty remarks were known to me as I was often the target of bullying. When Mr. Branch walked back into the room, everything returned to normal. He disciplined those whose names were on the board. The experience was effective as I began to understand what it takes to be a leader. I had to reconsider the taped message recorded in my inner life, at a young age, that I might not be good enough to lead.

My childhood friend, Kim Wilson, told me one day, "You are going to be a preacher when you grow up." We were probably in fifth or sixth grade. I said, "No, I am going to be a secretary." What high aspirations for a career! During my senior year in high school, the Whitehaven District Association, an organization of Baptist churches, offered an annual oratorical contest for high school seniors with a grand prize of five hundred dollars to go towards college tuition. I called Glenda Baskin Glover, now President of Tennessee State University, and shared my desire to enter the contest. The theme of the contest was, "Building a Foundation for Christian Education." I remember the four points: worship, prayer, study, and fellowship. Glenda helped me prepare for the moment. She said, "You memorize it, and I am going to show you how to preach it." And that she did!

On the day of the contest, there were only two candidates—me and another student who did not show up. The Association gave me the five-hundred-dollar scholarship. I really thought I was going to get out of saying the speech. But they encouraged me to give my speech. When I finished, they said, "You would have won anyway." That was in 1978. Nineteen years later, Pastor Alvin O'Neal Jackson hired me in the role of Associate Pastor of Christian Education at Mississippi Boulevard Christian Church (MBCC). The same preacher who preached the sermon that led me to surrender to the call would eventually become my pastor, Rev. Dr. Frank A. Thomas at MBCC. I had responsibility for ninety Sunday School classes and close to one hundred and fifty teachers (we believed in co-teachers). I developed teacher training curriculum and selected and coordinated studies in partnership with teachers for children and adults from the cradle to the grave.

My college choice led me to the University of Tennessee at Martin, a public, predominantly White university in Northeast Tennessee. I received Pell grants and took out student loans to pay for my tuition. I remember taking a communications course as an elective (I wish someone would have told me to major in it). Each student had to write a five-minute speech and share it in class from the speaker's podium. I spoke on the subject, "Capital Punishment is Wrong," and laid out my points through the scripture reference, "Thou shall not kill." At the end of the speech, a male White student came up to me and affirmed my oral presentation. However, he said, "I wish I had time to tell you why capital punishment is not wrong." Looking back, I wish we would have taken the time to hear each other out. In the 1980s, White students did not dialogue with Black students on campus. We all kept to our circles. This school was not kind to Black students on a broader scale. However, we did the best we could.

Calculus was not kind to me either. After taking it a second time during summer school, I was in community with a group of Black students trying to get a decent grade so that we could graduate. The instructor offered no support. He intentionally lectured to the White side of the room. However, the Black students came together, studied together, and made it out of the class. I graduated with a bachelor's degree in office administration.

The Call

My call to ministry evolved in August 1992. I remember talking to another friend a couple of days before that third Sunday on Raines Road. She voiced on numerous occasions that she was not called into ministry. I was not sure, but I knew something was going on in my inner spiritual world. After broken relationships, I gave God my heart. I served in almost every ministry in the church. Loving church people came later. I wanted this God that MBCC shared with me Sunday after Sunday. I told my friend "I'm going to keep running." We laughed it off and kept shopping. That Sunday, Rev. Thomas visited MBCC to preach. At that time, he was the pastor of New Faith Baptist Church in Chicago. Pastor Jackson would often invite guest preachers for special programs and events at the church or to fill the pulpit when he was away. The church was still located on Raines Road, getting ready to relocate to Bellevue Boulevard in Midtown Memphis.

This particular Sunday, Pastor Thomas' sermon title was "Lord, See My Change," the story of Naaman the Leper (II Kings 5). In the text, a servant girl had the solution to Naaman's leprosy. She urged him to go see the prophet, Elijah. The message for Naaman was to go and wash in the Jordan River seven times. I resonated with his dilemma. I had my own identity as a person with leprosy. Having dealt with atopic dermatitis all my life, I excluded myself from school activities. I was bullied because of my appearance and restricted in physical activities. I was invisible. I normalized it because it kept me safe from rejection. Do you know what made the difference? I was intelligent, witty, and bold.

While Pastor Frank preached, I thought about sitting on the stage at an honors program at Graves Elementary in the sixth grade. I made the honor roll and won second place in the spelling bee. In my mind, I felt eyes staring at me curiously, as if to say, "Why is she up there? She is ugly, but she must be smart." Every time Pastor Frank proclaimed what happened to Naaman when he went down into the water, I thought I was the one going down into the water, being washed and cleansed from the ugliness within my beauty. On the third dip, through the fourth dip and the fifth dip and through the sixth dip, something was stirring. On the seventh dip, I had to do something. By the seventh dip, I began to pace back and forth in front of my seat. I finally made my way down the aisle.

I heard the spirit of the Lord speak to me, "Give me your life, Nadine. Give me the rest of your life today." (I am taking a break here to dry my tears). Rev. Shirley Prince saw me struggling. She came, took my hand, and said, "Come on, baby, I already know." My life changed that day. I went home and told my parents that I accepted a call into ministry. My daddy responded, "I need to sit down" (that's another story). My family supported me from that day on. We had discussions regarding women being called to preach but not called to be a pastor. I had a meeting with Pastor Jackson. I asked him why God was calling me to do this. I told him I was not worthy to serve God and the church in this way. He told me, "Ms. Nae, none of us are worthy. God makes us worthy."

In 1992, my career path began to shift from human resources to the path of ordained ministry. In 1988, I started as a secretary at Sharp Electronics and was promoted to Human Resources Generalist after one year. Before that, I was a secretary at St. Jude Children's Research Hospital in Pharmacy and

Pharmacokinetics. Transitioning from my secular career to working in full-time ministry took five years from initially answering the call to ministry to working full-time at MBCC. After I accepted the call, I continued to work at Sharp Electronics while attending Memphis Theological Seminary part-time at night. Sharp refused to pay for my seminary education. They said that it did not align with their organizational goals. Faithfully, I took out another student loan after having recently paid off my student loan from college.

The skills I developed at Sharp Electronics transferred beautifully to administrative work in ministry. The Japanese executives at Sharp taught me a one-hundred-and-fifty-percent work ethic, with a commitment to detail and excellence. However, my hunger and heart began to search for God. I became a preacher, pastor, administrator, counselor, teacher, chaplain, and prayer warrior, and not all in that order. I was ordained in December 1997. I started working full-time at MBCC and used my skills to organize filing systems and coordinate the work of the Christian Education Commission and built a solid team. I organized our team's $100,000 annual budget and developed yearly goals for our Christian Education program. Pastor Thomas shared during one staff meeting, "This is one of the best-run Christian Education Commissions that I have seen in a long time." He and the other pastors asked me, "How do you do it?" I shared that I spent time with my people. We met, fellowshipped, strategized, and put goals in place for our ministry together. You see, it wasn't just me. It was a team of volunteers who loved God and loved educating God's people—Rev. Dr. Jackie Wilborn, Rev. Sheila Easterling-Smith, Norma Hunt, Kenneth Hughes, Elder Laverne Bobo, Charles Boone, and so many others.

Pastoral Identity

I was shaped for ministry by a dedicated group of colleagues and mentors: Glenda Glover, Elizabeth Haynes, Elizabeth Durham, Bessie Nathaniel, all Sunday School teachers from Mt. Pisgah Missionary Baptist Church. My sister, Denise Alexander, was and continues to be my rock and advocate, giving me wisdom through the years. Rev. A.C. Jackson, Pastor Alvin Jackson, Rev. Dr. Frank Thomas, Rev. Shirley Prince, Rev. Celeste Williams, Rev. Dr. Cozette Garrett, Rev. Dr. Stacey Spencer, Rev. Melvin Gross, Rev. Dr. Denise Bell, Rev. Dr. Jackie McHenry and others were willing to sit with me and answer my questions, and they challenged me to embrace a pastoral identity when I barely understood the implications of the call. These men and women were my examples. They experienced God calling them by name, and they never let me justify not being good enough to not follow the call.

There was a group of us who were groomed for ministry together at MBCC. We found ourselves in prayer meetings on Wednesday nights with Elder Charles Boyle and Saturday morning intercessory prayer meetings with Tread and Epsie Baird, followed by Pastor Jackie McHenry. We attended Wednesday night worship services, women's retreats, and twenty-four-hour prayer vigils, where we fasted all day and into the night. I remember one prayer vigil in particular. It was three o'clock in the morning. We walked on spiritual waters! Signs and miracles were performed in that prayer vigil. God worked in us and changed our lives and formed us for service in the church. We attended twenty-six-week new member classes. We were shaped in the Disciples of Christ identity within the African American context of church life. This is important to note because there were and still are diverse ethnic and cultural contexts for church life, identity, and community outside of the dominant, White patriarchal identity of the Disciples of Christ.

Pastoral identity and ethics in ministry were attributes with which I struggled. In 1999, it was easy for me to ask my ministry supervisor the ethics of pulpit attire and attire beyond the pulpit for African American women ministers. Jokingly I asked, "Why can't I wear my Daisy Dukes?" In the past, I would never have had the notion or intention of wearing anything that would expose my body. In my newfound freedom, shaped for ministry, I asked, "But why can't I wear them?"

My ministry supervisor responded, "You can't wear them in Memphis. You have to go to Atlanta and wear them, where nobody knows you are a pastor!" We laughed it off.

However, there was something much deeper the Spirit wanted to teach me. Who am I going to be inside and outside of the church, in my public life and my private life? Can I be a Black woman, be human, be loved physically and intimately, and be an ordained minister?

There was layer upon layer that I had to put on and take off, both spiritually and emotionally, at the same time. One of my favorite scriptures is, "For you formed my inward parts; you covered me in my mother's womb. I will praise you, for I am fearfully and wonderfully made." (Psalm 139:13–14). I had purpose in the Lord, far beyond what I understood then. Today, I have the freedom to process and be free, to question and be free, to engage the woman in me and not deny her as I show up in the world. I have the scars to show the world that norms don't define me. I was never normal.

As the Minister for New Church Leader Development with New Church Ministry and Church Extension, I discerned the gifts in God's people, when they had the gifts to plant a church, and when they were not called to plant but had a desire to. I am an advocate for equality and for the ways God wants to use all of us collectively as the Body of Christ. It was a wonderful opportunity to work with our Hispanic, Black, White, Asian, Pacific Islander, and LGBTQ constituency groups. That much power in one room transformed, empowered, and set our hearts on fire. I drafted my thesis for my doctorate in ministry on the subject, "Considering the Multicultural Reality Within the Christian Church (DOC)." If we want to be who we say we are, then we need a new language, a language of the spirit, where all are heard, empowered, and given the freedom to be the body of Christ.

In 2009, I was worn out, grief stricken from the passing of my mother, and exhausted from finishing a doctorate in ministry degree at Lexington Theological Seminary. I did not have time to grieve my mother's death because my proposal was due two months after she passed away in 2008. Two weeks before graduation in 2009, a lady rear ended me. My health started to decline. I left Church Extension in 2011. By the end of that year, I had five surgeries known only to my inner circle. Speculations abounded about my departure from Church Extension. "Is she ill? Is she having mental issues? Is she an alcoholic?" The best thing about my sabbatical, which is a gift from the church, is that it allowed me to be still long enough to hear God say in 2010, "You know you can go home and heal." This is what I chose to do. And God made provisions for me to be able to heal.

I wanted to quit the church. I thought I would quit. I went back to Memphis and sat down for a year and a half, and no door opened for me. I said, "I can go back to Human Resources and be a secretary or administrator," but no door opened. That was the situation until MBCC gave me an interim position, that allowed me to return to parish ministry. I felt tears rising again.

Going back to MBCC was different from when I worked there in the late nineties. It was a new culture with a new pastoral staff. The old guard was gone, and a new guard was in place. The new pastors invited me to dinner. When I arrived, one of them said, "We are going to let you back into the pastor's club." I said OK, but of course it bothered me. A week later, I was processing with a friend. I kept telling her, "He said they are going to let me back into the pastor's club." Finally, something within me said, "Wait a minute, I am the club!" I said, "Girl, the Lord said I Am the club."

As I shared this with my friend, she said, "You need to put that on a t-shirt and sell it." The "I am" in me needs no invitation. The "I am" in me is the club of inclusion, my identity, and my all-rightness in my transition and uncertainty of my future. I finally landed an interim position that led to the settled position as the Executive Regional Minister for the Great River Region of the DOC.

Today, I confront head-on images of power that do not include Black women. When I walk into a room, I bring a presence. That's who "I am." People can deny my skin color and my gender, but they cannot deny when Nadine Burton walks into the room with the power and presence of God. That's how I confront it. It is intimidating for some people. However, God has given me grace, kindness, and patience. I have learned to love on people, to receive them, and to not take them too fast where they may not be ready to go. That image of power always takes me back to who "I am" as an African American woman—Black, beautiful, bold, articulate, and a lover of the word of God. It's not on me to defend the power within me. It is on those around me to understand and embrace this woman God called for this moment in history. Amen, somebody. It has taken me sixty-five years to get here.

As I have aged, I have grown soft. My physical exteriors and walls are broken. God removed my stony heart and gave me a heart of flesh. The words of Parker Palmer in, "A Journey Toward an Undivided Life" deepened my self-awareness and the gravity of my spiritual transformation. He says, "Integrity is the state of being entire, complete, and unbroken...deeper still, integrity refers to something...in its unimpaired, unadulterated, or genuine state, corresponding to its original condition." Thinking back on my journey, I had to make some difficult decisions regarding friendships and relationships in deciding to live for and become a follower of Jesus Christ and to walk with integrity into my call. Every day is a struggle. Every day I renew my yes, because "all of the promises of God in him are yes and amen." I keep changing and evolving, knowing what I want and what I do not want in my life, in relationships, and my work ethic. Wow! There's a steady pace now, there is wisdom now to look back over my life and see how grace shaped, formed, and brought me thus far.

My work with the African American Female Regional Ministers Support Group began when I worked as the Executive Regional Minister for the Great River Region. Regional Ministry is one of the most difficult assignments in the Christian Church (DOC). I learned over the last five years to be open to the spirit of God doing new things in me. I had difficulty fitting into women's groups. I eventually let my guard down to embrace the nurture and care of these women. I learned to show up, to be vulnerable and transparent. Now I can say I am part of a women's group. I have not been able to say that for the majority of my almost thirty years in ministry. I hope this group stays together, prays together, and continues to celebrate our joys and challenges as a community. They are my sisters.

Today, as I near retirement, I pray for our church to be resilient, to be able to weather the changes that are coming - changes that we now face with the rollback of civil rights, education, healthcare, and climate change. I want everyone to work as hard as I do, but that may not be fair. It's important to just do the best that you can do for the Body of Christ. Give your best. Or, as Pastor Thomas taught his staff, "Do the right things in all relationships." Am I asking too much for leaders to be accountable and to give and be the best that we can, so that the Body of Christ can thrive together?

The more we live and work in ministry, the more questions we need to ask each other as it relates to our covenant together. Questions open the way for new revelations different from where we were three years ago, five years ago, or twenty years ago. Questions move us to resurrection, as we give old traditions permission to die, as we lay some things down and pick up new ideas and strategies that will encourage us to live on and be the church. Parker Palmer asserts that if we can live in the tension of this reality and not jump ship on each other, we may come to know a third way, which can help us to live into new realities of being church.

Wisdom for the Next Generation

I hope there are full circle moments that will help you contemplate your future leadership. May you be surrounded by God, church, and community. The same God in Joshua chapter one is the same God who leads Nadine Burton and is the same God who can inspire, direct, transform and lead you home.

What wisdom can I leave for the next generation of leaders? Take care of yourself spiritually, emotionally, physically, and holistically. Bring your best self to the table. When you bring your best self, God does his best work. When we are broken and confused, we may lose our way. There are times when we have to come away with God to refocus and get our direction and center our life back to the Spirit of God within us. As I consider the stories of my sisters presented in this book, I affirm for myself: We are not called to do this work alone. I encourage you to find your group. Let them teach you how to be an excellent leader, leading with strategic vision, collaboration, intentionality, and persistence. When you fall, get back up. When you waver, find your way back to God. When you want to give up, watch where the Spirit will lead you when you surrender to God's will for your life, and embrace the surrender. Because if you belong to God, you are never outside of the Lord's reach! I invite you with the spirit of boldness to consider how you might:

- Confront images of power with integrity, clarity, and grace.
- Speak up with the love and wisdom that God gives you.
- Never give in to anxiety, fear, or isolation.
- Keep people around you that will challenge you to become the best version of yourself.
- Balance your faith, work, and life journey.
- For single ministers, you are a family of one. Take care of your family.
- Do the best that you can for your church and community, but don't let it kill you.
- Lead out of your integrity, character, and a willingness to show people the way.

A Final Word

God of grace and mercy, I thank you for full circle moments that represent your presence and victory in me. I love that you love me unconditionally. I love that your power lives in me. I pray that these stones may become bridges for African American female leaders, and all leaders who love and serve you with all their heart as they love their neighbor. Thank you. In Jesus' name, Amen.

— ***Rev. Dr. Nadine Burton*** *is the first African American woman to serve as the Executive Regional Minister of the Christian Church in the Great River Region. She serves the Great Lakes Zone of the Christian Church Foundation as a vice president.*

The Village Is Undefeated

Surrounded by Faith

Rev. Dr. Dara Cobb Lewis

God Called This Woman

I am a double pastor's kid. Both my parents are ministers, so for most of my life I have seen my mother, Susie Holman Cobb, robe up and lead in congregational worship. I accompanied her when she took communion to homebound congregants. I sat on nearby chairs as my mom sat by the bedside of the sick and dying and offered prayers. I knew of the times when she left the house late at night because someone in the community was in distress. She'd stepped toward conflict with only God's angels and the Holy Spirit within her for protection. I've heard her asking for God's presence and power to be made known in all circumstances.

This was the village in which I was raised. My mother taught me that women minister. Not *can* minister. My mama taught me that women *minister*. She taught me by what she said and didn't say and what she did and didn't do as a woman of the cloth.

On November 6, 1977, my mother became the first African American female ordained in the Christian Church (Disciples of Christ) in South Carolina. It wasn't an easy journey. She had to deal with people telling her women should not be in ministry. Not everyone believed that, but it sometimes seems the naysayers not only held the microphone but also enjoyed using it.

Around this time, my mother started wearing dresses and skirts all the time. This was one of the easier concessions for people who believed they knew what was best for women in ministry. In those dresses, she kept preaching with fire, sharing the love of God and offering compassion to those in need. Sometimes with words and other times with silence, she taught generations of women that women minister.

My parents answered a call to start a church in Columbia, South Carolina. At the time, I was a rising sophomore in high school. I did not want to move away from the small town where I had lived for so long. It was filled with relatives and the only friends I had ever known. My dear grandparents lived there. But my parents were faithful to the call of Jesus Christ.

I cried myself to sleep for weeks. It was during one of those weeping nights that I heard God calling me. As I prayerfully shared with God how mad and sad I was that my parents had moved me to Columbia, I clearly understood God telling me that I had to move away to do the ministry God was calling me to do. In so many ways, fifteen-year-old me could hardly care less. In fact, I did not answer this call until I was 27. I knew the cost and sacrifice of answering God's call. I'd seen my parents do it. I postponed it as long as I could.

Coming to terms with my call was a long journey filled with opportunity and support. I was the president of the youth in my last two years of high school. As I college freshman and sophomore, I was the adult adviser for the statewide Christian Youth Fellowship. I took them on retreats to the mountains, sponsored basketball tournaments, and led them on a trips to the International Christian Youth Fellowship.

So when I finally yielded to the call and went to seminary, imagine my surprise when I encountered people who believed God did not call women into ministry. It was 1999 and I did not expect to find that the concept of women in ministry would need to be aggressively defended. We're not even talking about a woman being called to lead a congregation (or more likely to be an associate or assistant minister at a congregation). Given my upbringing, a female clergyperson seemed to be a no-brainer in 1999.

Seminary was inclusive of many denominations. People of many races, ethnicities, and backgrounds attended and it was more liberal than me. While some of the concepts taught were new to me, learning just how negatively some people saw female clergy caught me off guard. People told my colleagues and me to our faces their thoughts of women in ministry. They loved quoting Paul's admonishment that, "women should keep quiet in the church." I pushed ahead with assurance and graduated with my Master of Divinity degree. I was going to do what God had called me to do.

Today, I infrequently encounter people who believe women should not be ministers. However, from time to time it can be an obstacle for me. My experience and my village taught me that this obstacle is surmountable.

Me Too in Ministry

While most of my fellow seminarians were preparing for congregational ministry, I felt a pull to serve God overseas. As a younger African American woman, I was excited to serve in Africa. I was aware that compared to other demographics in mainline Protestant churches, not many African Americans showed interest in serving in overseas ministries.

On my day of ordination, I was also commissioned to be a mission coworker in Southern Africa. I had completed Mission Week, where I learned what to expect as a mission coworker. During Mission Week, I met some men that were affiliated with the ministry where I would serve, which led me to feel more connected to my ministry assignment. I met fellow mission coworkers. I connected with a particular mission coworker. We did what many people attending a conference do; we shared meals, sat beside each other in meetings and became fast friends. She is older and we would serve at locations approximately five hours apart. I value her wisdom.

When I arrived at my mission assignment, I was thrilled. I was to serve as sort of an associate executive minister working closely with the General Minister of a local denomination. I was very excited as this was my first place of service as an ordained minister, and I was hopeful about how God would use me in this place.

To my eyes, the country of my assignment was beautiful. It is semi-arid, and the trees were sparse. The dirt in the city where I was placed was fine, dark red sand. That particular sand got everywhere and like beach sand clings to you. I wanted to explore the city and outlying areas. Many of the people I encountered were kind and welcoming. I got along well with the people who worked in the office and became friends with one of the volunteers. While humorous, my biggest concern was a Kentucky Fried Chicken (KFC) a couple of doors from the office. I thought that KFC was too close to the office for me to remain healthy.

It started almost immediately, but because I was in another country with different cultural norms, I was unsure if I was assessing the situation properly. The little hairs on the back of my neck were telling me I should be wary. First, I noticed that my hand was being held a little past my comfort zone. Yet when I looked around, it seemed that many people held hands. I hadn't been there long enough to be able to tell if longer handholding was between female friends, male friends, romantic partners, or male/female friends. I just saw longer handholding than what I was familiar with in the United States. But when he held my hand, it just felt too long, and that made me squeamish.

There were other things, like brushing up against my body by reaching across the car to release my seat belt without asking me and before I could do it myself. I began to feel more uncomfortable. This was not someone who could be avoided in my assigned role. Following a work trip to a rural village, cultural norms aside, I became more alarmed by behavior that was increasingly an issue for me.

One day, I was touched in a way that removed doubt. The behavior was not cultural, and men and woman did not interact as friends, coworkers, or church members in this way. I had been touched inappropriately by someone who had authority over me. He had keys to the house where I would begin living in a few days. I was anxious about how things could escalate and about the level of care, safety, and support being provided. Though I had contacted my sending ministry, things were not moving as quickly as necessary for me to be safe. I did not feel a sense of urgency on their part. I was unsure if they saw the situation as a dangerous one, because that was not communicated to me.

I was grateful when my friend from Mission Week reached out to our sending ministry to advocate for me. She told them that they should imagine what it would feel like if I was one of their daughters. Then she said, "Send her to me." Those words will stay in my heart forever. I was sent to her. I felt safe. I thank God with every remembrance I have of her. What a village God has given me.

Feeling Lonely in Ministry

There is an epidemic of loneliness in the world right now. It came into stark light during the COVID-19 pandemic when so many of us were forced into our homes for physical health. I say physical health because for many, whether they lived alone or with others, it deeply impacted their mental health. Solitude is one thing. It can feel like an empowered choice. Loneliness is entirely another thing. It can feel like a weight around one's neck, pulling you down to the ground.

Loneliness can look like a person who is sick and in need of care with no one to drive them home from the hospital. It can look like having no one with whom to give thanks, so a person eats a peanut butter and jelly sandwich in their bed on the fourth Thursday in November. It can look like a famous singer who falls ill or dies in their home, and no one discovers their body for weeks.

Loneliness can look like a pastor who is surrounded by many people on Sunday morning and throughout the week but is still lonely. I experienced this while serving a church in the 2000s. I was involved in the life of the church. I planned many programs for youth and adults. I led mission trips every year. I organized retreats. I participated in programs in the region where I served and on a national level in the general church of my denomination. I went to many galas and fundraisers in the community. I served on boards in our city, region, and the general church. I was invited into the homes of members from time to time. Yet I was profoundly lonely. I went home to an empty house for many hours a day. I made a few friends through church but not with many people in the community. Interestingly, I don't think anyone noticed my loneliness.

Had it not been for the preexisting people in my village, I would have abandoned the call I had at that church before God had given me the green light to move. Having a village that held me in its loving embrace at a time when I felt invisible even while leading many people made a huge difference in my life.

While I know there are footprints in the sand showing when God carried me, if I pay attention and take a second look, I will see that there are several other footprints where faithful sisters in Christ carried me also. My village is undefeated.

Driving Across North Carolina

In 2018, I was diagnosed with breast cancer and thus began a life-changing part of my journey. Soon after this diagnosis, genetic testing revealed I have the BRCA 1 gene mutation that makes me more susceptible to certain types of cancer. I underwent radiation and several surgeries, some to address the current cancers and others elective. It was a hard time for me and my loved ones. We stood as strong as we could. There were friends and family who were with me at surgeries and some radiation appointments. They hosted social events to let me know I was not alone and I was loved.

One event stood out to me. There was a minister who quietly collected items from the Disciples Women groups from across the state. Then she drove with those items for hours until she reached me. When she did, she showed once again that my village is strong and included more sisters than I imagined. I was so taken aback. She hugged me and said this was simply the goodness that I'd put out into the world returning to let me know how much I meant to many people. It was such a good reminder that the village that relies on me is one that I can also rely on.

A Tethered Ministry

In 2010, I got married. Into our marriage I brought a son and a daughter, and he brought two sons and a daughter. Together we continued to raise the youngest three children, who were then in third, fourth, and fifth grade.

During this time, I felt led to tether my ministry to the Charlotte, North Carolina area. There were times when I flirted with moving to another area of the country to serve a ministry. This often occurred when someone told me of an open ministerial position for which they thought I'd be a good candidate. Sometimes they'd already recommended me to a search committee. When this happened, I'd research the position. On a few occasions, I explored an opening to see what would happen. However, I knew in my heart that Charlotte was homebase. The kids were in school, and we were close to family, friends, and a church community. It made sense to stay.

I went back to seminary to pursue a Doctor of Ministry in Pastoral Care and Counseling. My research project was on the use of spiritual practices for the treatment of anxiety and depression in religiously serious women. Following my graduation and completion of the requirements of the North Carolina Board of Fee-Based Practicing Pastoral Counselors, I became an NC-certified pastoral counselor. In this work, I take an integrative approach, using the behavioral sciences combined with spirituality, theology, and the person's religious experience to work towards health and wholeness. I seek to make my services affordable by accepting insurance and sometimes offering a sliding fee scale.

I had imagined I would spend the bulk of my ministry in congregations. I felt the same way when I left overseas ministry. God had shown me that God could and would lead me from one type of fulfilling ministry to the next. It turned out to be true with pastoral counseling as well.

I'd been resistant to the idea of tethering to one area. I liked the freedom of turning up anywhere I wanted to serve God. I have an exploring spirit. That is the part of me that God used to lead me to my overseas mission work. I did not easily embrace the idea of seeing myself in the same area for more than a decade, but I accepted it. The tethered work God called me to as a pastoral counselor is fulfilling. I share parts of the gospel daily. I deconstruct theology weekly. I introduce many people in my practice to womanist thought. This empowers individuals to rethink harmful ways of considering their value, life experiences, and trauma. They no longer demonize anxiety and depression because of the ways mental health issues have been taught in their communities and churches. They don't see themselves as weak Christians because they struggle with a mental health disorder. They recognize that the many people they see everyday struggle with some challenge.

Sometimes when people ask me how I serve in ministry these days, I notice an air of dismissiveness, as if what I do is not ministry. Perhaps they don't understand the call of a pastoral counselor. The service offered is hard, meaningful, and potentially life-changing work for clients. It is hard, meaningful, and life-changing work for me. This is ministry. Unless God tells me differently, I am tethered to it.

Sharing Joy

God has used me throughout my ministerial vocation to serve in various ways. Some of those ways have been more visible than others, and some of those calls have been seen as having a value that is assumed to be a higher achievement. When that happened and I wanted to celebrate it with friends, it is not always as possible as I would have liked. When I received my doctorate degree, opened my practice as a pastoral counselor, or became a Regional Minister, not everyone I love celebrated these things with me. These are achievements. They were not handed to me on a gold platter. They came with a lot of hard work and sacrifice. The doctorate degree came with trips from Charlotte, North Carolina to Louisville, Kentucky a few times annually for over four years. I studied while raising my family. I had to do a research project and defend it. I did this while working full-time to contribute to the support of my household.

To become a pastoral counselor certified by the state of North Carolina, I had to complete specialized training, which I did through my studies to earn a Doctor of Ministry in Pastoral Care and Counseling. In addition, I had to complete at least 1,375 hours of direct client counseling with a minimum of 250 hours supervised by an experienced senior pastoral counselor. By the grace of God, I did that. I had to successfully pass a written and an oral examination. Every year I must complete 50 hours of continuing education.

Opening my private practice was one of the biggest leaps of faith I have ever taken. When I left the place where I was a contracted therapist, I did not know if I would be able to continue to contribute to my family the way I always had. I did not know how long it would take me to build a client caseload that would sustain me. I did not know if I would have to return to my former place of work with my tail between my legs. I believed and hoped that my dream could be a reality. I trusted God. With the encouragement of my husband, family, and friends, I started with only five clients. Eventually I built a thriving practice with a waiting list. Thanks be to God.

No gold platter. These things were accomplished through lots of prayer, hard work, and sacrifice.

One of the saddest commentaries about life is that people often realize that they don't have anyone with whom to share their joys. They may be achieving one of their biggest dreams and are so proud of themselves that they feel like they can burst. Yet they withhold or downplay their achievement because they don't know if their close friends will celebrate with them from an authentically good place.

One of the best things I have ever seen on social media is a video of a sixteen-year-old girl who is at the end of her dance class and it's her birthday. She is about to call her parents to pick her up. Her friend says the girl's parents had to go somewhere but dropped something off for her. The friend then hands her a set of keys. The birthday girl begins to scream. The whole room of about 12 girls erupts into screams and cheers with her. As the girl runs from the building, disoriented because she does not know where she is going, her best friend leads the way as the rest of girls follow, all experiencing the euphoria of the moment. When the girl gets into the car—her car—she begins to hit the steering wheel with extreme happiness. The other girls yell with happiness for her. The birthday girl looks in the mirror, smooths her hair behind her ear, flicks her head up with an expression that defies being fully explainable, and starts her car. Then she screams and is again joined by the other girls.

I can't tell you how much I love this video! Every time I share it with someone I love, I think everyone should have friends like this. I am grateful that I have friends like the girls in my village. I can call them with my big and small achievements, and they cheer me. I can hear the girl in these women jumping up and down with exuberance that their friend has done the thing. Likewise, I cheer them on. No envy. No jealousy. They mean so much to me.

I heard someone in my village say to someone else that they were so happy for a younger person's achievement. The older person said that they could not have dreamed of doing something like the young person was doing. When the older person was younger, life was so different. So the older person was joyous and proud to see this adventurous and freeing ambition the younger person pursued. No envy or insincere or feigned compliments. Just love and pride shared for a fellow villager. We all need friends and family members like that.

You're Doing Too Much

I have found that one of the biggest enemies of a thriving ministry is doing too much. When we begin to show up in certain spaces and people recognize our value, people will want us to serve in one way or another. Maybe it's the flattery that entices us or maybe we never learned how to say no when it is against our best interests. Maybe we didn't understand or we resist boundaries. One day we looked up from all of the yeses and find ourselves surrounded by messes. Our calendars are overbooked. We are past tired. We are not doing our best anywhere because we are everywhere at the same time.

I have found myself in that place more than once. People like to quote the saying, "I'm too blessed to be stressed." However, in a place like the one I previously described, it is easy to feel "too stressed to feel blessed" to be in all those meetings, on all those boards, and with so many people waiting on something from you.

I experienced this unsettling way of functioning early in ministry. I was on about five boards and committees. Some were local; others were national. I worked full-time. It was too much. In many full-time church ministries, many pastors or associate pastors already struggle to keep their work within 40 hours a week. When you include all those other commitments, it can easily become too much to handle.

That way of being is harmful for our mental, physical, and spiritual health. When we are stressed from overcommitment, we may become irritable. Our physical health suffers. We find ourselves with high blood pressure or putting on weight. Our spiritual practices are negatively affected. We become anxious. On the outside, we try to produce at a level that passes for high-quality work. People even be satisfied. Yet *we* are dissatisfied. We are exhausted and unhappy. Our interior lives suffer. At this point, positive self-talk assists us in making changes in our own best interests.

At my best, I manage my yeses and my noes more responsibly. I leave plenty of space in my calendar for my family. I attend to my healthcare needs as the priority they should be. I have time for my friends. I make time to do nothing. I am the queen of self-care. My boundaries are a thing of beauty. This is how things are at my best.

But if I let my boundaries erode, I will find myself right back in the place where I am overextended. I'll say yes beyond my ability to perform at the capacity I would like to offer. I will squeeze out including other, more meaningful things that I would like to focus on. I will also not give space for someone with more time and energy to say yes to participating in a ministry that they may have been praying for someone to offer them.

In a healthy village, we hold each other accountable. My fellow villagers have permission to hold me to my goals for self-care. My commitment to my village and to myself is that I hear them and consider what they are saying so that I can reset my priorities. I try not to be defensive but rather embrace what my village says for my well-being, because I believe that in this place I am loved and cared for.

This is an ongoing assessment for me. I ask myself if I am living in a balanced way that contributes to my overall well-being. I ask myself why I said yes to one thing and no to another. I ask myself if I have left enough space in my life to be as present for my villagers as I need them to be present for me.

Who Are Your People?

Many of my formative years were spent in Holly Hill, South Carolina. I lived there from the time I was four until I was almost fifteen. This is the hometown of my people, the Holmans. My mother returned home with her husband after living in other places. She had many relatives here. So I had the pleasure and privilege of growing up around and in daily contact with many cousins. Many of my relatives attended my church. My grandfather was an elder there, my grandmother was a deacon, and my parents were associate ministers.

Holly Hill is a small town with two stoplights and one grocery store, the Piggly Wiggly. With a current population of about 1,200, by some definitions it would be considered a village. So it's no wonder that when my grandparents met someone who a sibling or a cousin was dating, one of their first questions would be asked with a slight hint of a Gullah accent, "Who yo' people?" This question was not asked out of curiosity; it was a serious and practical question. It ensured that someone was not dating their cousin—and certainly not a close relative.

I have lived in several places since leaving Holly Hill. I have lived in places with a population much higher than Holly Hill. Briefly, I even lived in a place with 2.5 million people. The likelihood of dating a cousin was a minute possibility. Yet this serious and practical question—*Who yo' people?*—has accompanied me through my life because it is important to know who one's people are for a variety of reasons.

Wisdom for the Next Generation

1. Recognize your village. Discern who your people are.
2. Build your village as needed. Not everyone who starts in your village will remain there.
3. Your best has to be enough. Don't do too much.
4. Be well. Self-care is a necessity.

A Final Word

If we are open to the Holy Spirit, ministry can take us in many directions. As we faithfully follow where we are led, we are unsure about what we will meet when we arrive. There may be beauty beyond our wildest dreams. We may also encounter challenges that we never imagined. Finding your village is paramount. It is a foundational part of a successful ministry. Adding to your village as you answer different calls throughout your life is helpful. Your village will include those who will pray for and with you, shelter you, answer your call in the wee hours of the night, be a mentor to you, console you in the losses of life, and celebrate the high points of life with you. Be nurtured in your village. Nurture others in your village. Never think that you have gotten too big to need a village. At the end of the day, God and each other are all we have.

— ***Rev. Dr. Dara Cobb-Lewis*** *was the first African American woman to serve as the Regional Minister of the Christian Church in South Carolina and is a member of the Bethany Fellows Pastoral Leadership Initiative.*

An Ever-Flowing Stream

The Making of a River

Rev. Dr. Monique Crain Spells

The Village

In her book *The Theology of Mercy Amba Oduyoye*, Oluwatomisin Olayinka Oredein writes, "To understand someone's theology, we must first sit at the feet of a life." Long before I ever knew of the Christian Church (Disciples of Christ) or understood "call" as the discernible voice of God, there was an ocean of women who birthed me. I am their exotic river. My mother's grandmother, Winnie Mitchell, was a licensed hairdresser who graduated from Poro College of Cosmetology in 1918. This was the place where Madame C.J. Walker was equipped for her business empire. Winnie Mitchell was the mother of Lillian, Gertrude, Ruby, and Harold. My Great-Aunt Gertrude graduated from Howard University in 1944 with a degree in social work. My Great-Aunt Ruby worked for the Finance and Accounting Services Office of the Department of Defense, and my Grandmother Lillian was a student at Indiana University Extension in 1945, before marrying and mothering four children: Joseph, Jeffrey, Gerald, and my mother, Janice. Mama graduated with a bachelor's degree in elementary education from Purdue University, an M.Ed, and an M.S. in counseling from Indiana University. She was a trailblazing teacher during the bussing years when schools starting to desegregate. Mama and a few other teachers left Indianapolis Public Schools and followed Black children into predominantly white schools so that they could see themselves reflected in leadership. There has been a transgenerational current of education flowing through me since the day I was formed.

From my father's side, I have a great-grandmother named Annie Wright. A business owner and itinerant preacher, she sold timber from land that most thought could not turn a profit. Annie Wright was a land heir to her father who had run away from enslavement on a plantation in Hinds County, Mississippi. Our determined ancestor, Jacob Wright, reclaimed his freedom and went on to own over 600 acres of land in Grenada, Mississippi. As a single Black woman in the early 1900s, Annie Wright broke the mold. Preaching, playing well her hand, and marrying James Crain later than was usual age to marry at that time, she eventually birthed my grandfather Jacob Crain (named after her father) and his siblings. The legacy of Great-Grandmother Annie Wright's resourcefulness continued in my paternal great aunts Mary Crain Pollard and Addie B. Crain Willis. By way of the Great Northward Migration, along with my cousin, Maggie Crain, they owned and managed a total of twelve properties in Indiana. My father's sisters have humbly followed the stream. Annie Crain Cox owns five properties in Indiana and Rose Crain also owns multiple properties. These women were intentional about business, but their business leadership did not diminish their love for others. Family has always had a place to lay their head because of these women.

Proximity matters. It was the nearness of my Granddaddy's family land to the land where my father's mother, Veronia (pronounced Verona), worked in the cotton field that brought about the marriage of my grandparents. Grandmama gave birth to my dear father, Clarence Crain, and his older siblings, William, Thomas, Curtis, Annie, Rosie, and Louise. Veronia Williams Crain was the great-great granddaughter of Mariah, an enslaved Choctaw African American who birthed the son (George Willis) of her enslaver and hid him for several months (some say two years) to shield them both from the wrath of her enslaver's wife. Grandmama's mother, Courtney, married Daniel Williams and died young in childbirth, delivering the last of her children, a set of twin boys who also died. Grandmama's siblings (Eula, Havannah (Hay), Eunice, Hansen, Lee, Jeff, and Mel) lived in Grenada, Mississippi and Chicago. Aunt Eula and Aunt Hay owned farms down South with their husbands, and I am told that Aunt Hay was highly skilled in herbal healing. Although my grandparents moved to Indianapolis after Annie Wright died, we returned to my great aunts' homes in Mississippi every year, eating from the land with deep joy. I can remember as a child there were hogs at Aunt Hay's one season that were sausage in the next season…at least that is what Aunt Hay took delight in telling me during one visit. Characterized by housecoats, plaited hair, sun-kissed faces, overalls, long tables, pound cakes, canned preserves, chow chow, and incomparable collards, life down there was lived at a holy pace. It flowed with centuries of love. Moving to Indianapolis did not alter the Southern heart in my grandmother. She also grew vegetables in her backyard and had bottomless pots. Anyone who needed to eat could eat. From the time I was born until she became ill with brain cancer during my third-grade year, Grandmama's house was my other home, and her voice was the warmest blanket I have known on this side. There was never ugliness in the gaze of her family and household. Neither she nor her children are the bickering type, but I learned the influence of a glance, one's tone, and even silence. Those lessons live in my leadership today.

Embodied Values

My beginnings were ordered by embodied values in contrast to a world of trends. This explains why my life as a Black woman executive for God, my household, and the church are also ordered by embodied values. Love, learning, and resourcefulness were all around me, fueling upward from my roots. Still, it is important to name that my father has never once communicated a box of roles I should live into because I am female. Limitations did not exist in conversations related to my adult future, not from any familial direction, except that I must attend college or get out of the house.

As a kid, I played Little League shortstop, basketball, and was a cheerleader. My father, a basketball star himself, treated me, my twin sister, Monica, and my brother, Marques, like stars. His mantra was, "If no one will pass you the ball, create your own opportunity." When trigonometry started to shred my self-esteem, with loving authority and resolve, my father said, "If you did your best, that's the end of it." Mama was a praying woman who read books and wrote often, so I started writing in diaries when I was young. From watching her, it was clear to me writing was an escape from whatever stress came with the day.

While the freedom of womanhood dangled in the distance, there were quite a few expectations placed on my education, behavior, and body. I was raised not to embarrass myself or my family. I was raised to be respectful of leadership and hate no one. I was raised to know children all over the world had less to eat than I did, and gratefulness meant eating what I was offered, including my vegetables. I was raised to stay in "my place" among adults. And to no surprise, I was raised to be in a relationship with God. I can look back now and know that staying in "my place" never landed well with me. It created a tension that has thankfully worked for my good in ministry with others. Weekly time wrapped in Grandmama's love and enough understanding of Christian faith I had picked up from church helped me to understand that "my place" was much more expansive than what the law (Mama) allowed. I know my parents loved me and only wanted what was best for me, based on what they knew to be best. That meant trying to protect me from the world's pitfalls. Nonetheless, my voice was never crafted for silence. My emotions align with the movement of stars and the moon; they are irrepressible. They are measured but relentless in finding a portal and vessel. There were days when I wished I could be different, quieter, less curious, even less intelligent. The extraordinary gift of theological education helped me know those thoughts did not come from our Creator. Thanks be to God, I do not have such wishes anymore and have not for many years.

Advocacy, activism, and strategic pastoring in nontraditional religious settings have been divine paths for me to navigate becoming an authentic and effective faith leader. I studied at Purdue to be a journalist and an English teacher. By the time I reached the second semester of my first year, I was fighting for justice and staging a sit-in with 700 other students. We were demanding a new cultural center for African American students that was free of asbestos and lead and offered equitable bathrooms like the other campus buildings. Our demands were met because we were organized, collaborative, joyous, and committed. I left West Lafayette as a woman who had learned the power of a plan and the importance of deep regard for co-laborers. The contributions of others are always factored into the objectives and outcomes set for my ministry. Coming from a large family with the most amazing reunions, royal feast-like barbecues, and holiday pitch-ins, "the invisible institution" taught me there is too much to lose with any community endeavor by trying to go at it alone. I am reminded of my grandmother's cancer journey. My aunts and uncles took turns covering shifts so she could journey at home. This deep crisis never felt chaotic. It was terribly sad, yes, but never chaotic because the weight was being shared. It is holy wisdom to give and receive help. It is one of the greatest indicators of community. It is God incarnate.

From designing programs for military families to directing theater productions at peak womanhood, from mobilizing congregations around anti-racism as the Indiana Regional Moderator to planting Levi's Table, from curating compelling admissions experiences for seminarians to rehabbing Black Ministers Retreat as its first woman leader in 47 years of existence, these bright moments in ministry were communal victories that led to executive leadership in the church and effective team building. Genuine regard for the whole is a beautiful landing place in daily work. Ego is the quickest way to clip one's own wings, but the village is undefeated. I am a village woman with a village mindset. If Jesus was intentional to posse up, I should do the same as his follower.

This brings me to the grief of having a village mindset in predominantly white spaces of vocation that have traditionally been male-led. As a womanist theologian, my call carries with it an accountability around mutuality, authenticity, history, and liberated futures. There are seasons when every last one of those accountability factors feels under attack. American society was built on the backs of Black women who tended fields they did not own, nursed babies they did not birth, cleaned homes they did not live in, and cooked food they could not eat. This history created conscious and subconscious expectations of Black women to give and give and give without help while receiving little to nothing in return from the taker. I am not proud to say that I have done the work of two or three people for a fraction of what I should have been paid, as colleagues do a fraction of their one job and get paid generously. The masses know these facts. And yet it persists at great cost to health, family, intimate partnerships, retirement, and generational wealth.

Still, the call of God lingers at night and in the morning when all else is quiet. It tells me that God positioned me. It tells me not to faint and that reaping shall have its day. It tells me that those who really love God will also love me and help lift my arms. It tells me justice ain't a joke and God will not be mocked. It tells me to love people, not power, and to trust instinct over institution. It tells me that supernatural anointing is not the abandonment of my humanness but the embrace of it.

Giving no discount to the power and comfort of the Holy Spirit in my ministry, the inequity I have experienced in church-affiliated positions is saddening. The anemic, unspoken attitude that a Black woman is lucky to have an opportunity amidst dominant culture is palpable. This attitude implies that she does not belong and is a guest; we do not know her, so she should not lead us; she is liked in marketing material but not in authority; and her experience, expertise, credentials, and call are all irrelevant. These implications surface in disrespectful email correspondence, ignored instructions, missed deadlines, resignations, and other microaggressions simply in response to doing my job. Whenever these injuries occur, it comes to my mind quickly that I am not the first to have traveled this way. My ancestors have seen and endured unthinkable hardship in doing good for others. The ocean of women who poured down into me their exotic river would have never broken their stride over petty insults and shallow voyeurs. Neither have I; neither will I.

The Merriam-Webster dictionary defines an exotic river as "a stream (such as the Nile) that has its source in well-watered lands and crosses a desert on its way to the sea." The middleness of ministry has yet to take my eyes off the start and the finish of my call. For those who do not know when to shout hallelujah, this would be the time! Having little over a decade left in full-time ministry, I can say I have started to catch a glimpse of the sea off in the distance. I can smell it in the air and feel it on my skin. Poet and preacher's kid Margaret Walker authored the timeless poem *For My People in* 1942. It reaches my heart and brings it forward from behind the wall where it periodically retreats to survive sexism and racism in the church. It is the poem's last line (Let a race of men now rise and take control) that speaks to the fear some folk have of a Black woman's leadership. The fear that we might lead like those who came before us and never considered us, never programmed with us in mind, never resourced us well enough to thrive, never hired us is a real fear. I see it in the faces of those who only had to know someone from camp or college to get a job in the church. They know I did not have the hookup and yet, here I am, and it disorients them. I hope the fearful and disoriented know that I would never discount or undermine my call with ministry-crippling privilege. I would never put my comfort above communal good. My desire for a strong church seeks out practices and people who can help us all minister more like Jesus.

Wisdom for the Next Generation

- I am connected to the village that birthed me and inspired me. That village is both biological and chosen. Learn of your village. Learn its roots and also plant new ones that can strengthen you as you evolve. The Village is undefeated. No evil can overcome it.
- My values ground me as a leader and person. Stay in conversation with your values. Be accountable to them and do not betray them for ease. Protect them from disregard.
- Grief must have a safe place to land outside your body. Understand its vocational sources and establish healthy boundaries around those sources.
- Faith rooted in relationship with the Liberator-Jesus is necessary to cultivate progress. Jesus is leader of the church that I am called to serve.

A Final Word

For 24 years, I served in the middle of organizations, carrying out the priorities of my supervisors. They were all strengthened by my gifts and focus. It is good and right to reach executive leadership with an opportunity to cast strategic vision that has been held in prayerful discernment. The ever-flowing stream of faith and determination woven into my life has not ceased nourishing me. If

I could pass down a stream to emerging lakes, it would be to keep an eye out for Jesus. Keep an eye out for the markers of the Holy One.

Wherever you see light, love, justice, radical inclusion, food, shelter, advocacy, redemption, equity, and miracles anew, resource them! You will never regret decisions that support the embodiment of the Liberator-Jesus. Through it all, this is where your peace will come from—Living Water.

— ***Rev. Dr. Monique Crain Spells****, educator, author, clergywoman, is Vice President for Disciples Home Missions. She is the former moderator of the Christian Church in Indiana. Monique is mother to Niles.*

Reference

Oredein, O. O. (2023/2025). *The Theology of Mercy Amba Oduyoye: Ecumenism, Feminism, and Communal Practice.* University of Notre Dame Press

Walker, M. (1942). *For my people.* Yale University Press

Growing in the Margins
Searching for God

Rev. Joan Bell Haynes

Growing In the Margins: You Always Have Options
Look well to the growing edge. All around us worlds are dying and new worlds are being born; all around us life is dying and life is being born. The fruit ripens on the tree, the roots are silently at work in the darkness of the earth against a time when there shall be new leaves, fresh blossoms, green fruit. Such is the growing edge! It is the extra breath from the exhausted lung, the one more thing to try when all else has failed, the upward reach of life when weariness closes in upon all endeavor. This is the basis of hope in moments of despair, the incentive to carry on when times are out of joint and men have lost their reason, the source of confidence when worlds crash and dreams whiten into ash. The birth of the child—life's most dramatic answer to death—this is the growing edge incarnate. Look well to the growing edge!
— Howard Thurman Sermon, The Fellowship Church, San Francisco, CA 1947

A Grandmother's Love

I am the second daughter of Evelyn nee Wilson and Walter Bell Sr. When Mom and Dad had the opportunity to get away from the daily grind of life with seven kids to party with friends, they packed us up and walked us across the street to stay with our maternal grandparents. We frequently spent the night with them, because our parents came in long after midnight. The partying must have worn thin because I remember Gran saying to my parents, "I don't mind keeping my grandkids, but you had better come pick them up and take them home. I don't care how late it is!" Can you imagine being awakened out of your sleep as a child, carried across the street and up the hill at one or two o'clock in the morning? Mom was holding on to two us and Dad carrying the youngest. But during those sleepovers at my grandparents, I watched my beloved Gran on her knees praying. I never saw Granddaddy praying. Granted, he went to bed much earlier than Gran did. Perhaps he was too tired after working all day in the local lumber mill, where he lost his two middle fingers in a plant accident. It was my "fire baptized holiness" grandmother who gave me Jesus and the church. Not with scriptures, but by the way she practiced her faith. I watched her read her Bible and pray daily. I watched her love her family, work hard cleaning White peoples' homes (in fact, one of the women she worked for came to her home every Christmas with a gift after she retired). I watched my gran live her life as one of unconditional love, grace and beauty. I wanted to be like her when I grew up. She was beautiful inside and out. As a teenager, I would pray to have legs as pretty as hers, laughing out loud.

But I didn't want to go to her church.

It was the one known as the Fire Baptized Holiness Church of God. Yeah, that one. It scared me. Not because of its puritan restrictions: no jewelry except a cross around your neck, no dancing or listening to non-gospel music, no playing cards. No. No. No ad nauseam. The scriptures tell us God doesn't hear the prayers of sinners. "We know that God does not listen to sinners ..." – John 9:31a, NIV). However, I never heard part B of that scripture, "But he does listen to one who worships him and obeys his will." In my childhood brain, I was surely a sinner. I loved dancing, singing, and Marvin Gaye! I couldn't wait to meet him. Because I just knew if I met him, he would want to marry me at first look.

I was a sinner. I knew I was a sinner. So how would God hear my prayers? Would Jesus want to save me? How could I ever be like my grandmother if I was a sinner? How could God ever love me? Would I even have a chance? I loved my Gran. But I didn't like going to her church. In fairness to the memory of my grandfather, he was not a member of anybody's church, but every Sunday he drove my grandmother to church in his Ford pickup truck. He also drove his grandkids when my grandmother told my mom to get her children ready for Sunday School—which meant Sunday school and church, an all-day event. I went when Gran commanded us, but I didn't want to be there for those "sinners are going to hell" sermons. My escape route from that church was college away from home. Thank you, Jesus!

With a bachelor's in psychology from Albany State College I moved back home with my parents. I was the first in my family to receive a college degree. Having soaked in lots of words, ideas, and practices—some good, some not so good—I remember telling my mom I didn't believe that hell was a real place. It was a metaphor for being separated from God. Nor did I believe the devil was dressed in red walking around with a pitchfork in hand. I had been hanging out with poets and musicians who, like me, were shedding that layer of narrative that said we had to accept what we had been told by our families and the church. My mom looked at me and walked away. No words, just that look that said, "If I don't move away from her now, I will have to smack her." By then Mom had gone back to church, but not Gran's church. She had joined the Missionary Baptist tradition. I am sure she walked away praying for me not to go to hell. This is one reason why I love Dorothy Norwood's and Alvin Darling's gospel hymn:

Somebody Prayed For Me
Somebody prayed for me
Had me on their mind
They took the time and prayed for me
My mother prayed for me…(She had me on her mind)
had me on her mind
She took the time and prayed for me (Oh, yes, she did) (I'm so glad)
I'm so glad she prayed
…I'm so glad she prayed for me…
Jesus prayed for me. Always blessing me…
He took the time and prayed for me
(I'm mighty glad He prayed) I'm so glad He prayed…
I'm so glad He prayed for me…

I believe my mom's silent walking away was her way of giving me the space to discover my faith on my own terms. What a gift!

Over time, I discovered that the church of my mother and grandmother was not mine to have. Their faith was. But not their church. I had to find my own. I went through some church hurt, because I could not "be" in a church that did not welcome questions. It was a painful process finding a church that welcomed the totality of who I was. I searched for a faith community that could handle my questions about Jesus for a while without success. I finally stopped looking. In good time, the church came looking for me.

As I adjusted to living once again with my parents, I had to quickly decide whether to return to school for a master's degree or PhD, or get a job. I got a job in retail. Soon after, I moved to Atlanta at the invitation of friends I had met while working part-time during summer break. I was happy to receive a full-time paycheck. I eventually accepted an entry-level administrative position at Georgia State University in Atlanta. I loved being in the university setting and eventually landed a position that nurtured my yearning to guide college students in their careers. This set me on the path to becoming the assistant dean of Academics for the College of Health Sciences. I loved it! From 1978 to 1986, my life's goal was to work and become the best in my career, party (it is in my DNA, after all), fall in love, get married, and have two kids. The marriage-and-kids narrative didn't work out quite the way I planned.

An Invitation from a Stranger

In 1986 I received a phone call from a complete stranger who introduced herself as Rev. Cynthia L. Hale. She said she had been given my name and number by a co-worker, Charlotte Ivey, a member of First Christian Church in Decatur, Georgia.

Rev. Hale visited me in my office and shared her testimony and that she had been called to start a congregation for Black professionals in Atlanta. She invited me to join her for bible study in her home in Lithonia, Georgia. It was rare for me to meet someone my age that was excited about Jesus! Most of my contemporaries were "nones" in terms of practicing their faith. Church hurt can wound you for years if you let it. But I sensed deep spiritual roots in Rev. Hale that day and I agreed to attend the bible study.

Four people came to that first Wednesday evening study, all members of the Christian Church (Disciples of Christ), except me. One of those was Dr. Kenneth Henry, a professor at The Interdenominational Theological Center, a consortium of five predominantly African American denominational Christian seminaries in Atlanta. I was the only outsider (heathen) in the bunch. I had never heard of the Christian Church (Disciples of Christ) in the United States and Canada. But this woman pastor was feeding my soul with the knowledge of the Trinity: God, Jesus, and the Holy Spirit, through scripture, prayer and purpose. My mother and grandmother were worried I had fallen into a cult—seriously. Over time, I learned about Jim Jones and thought, well, their concerns were not completely unfounded. Once my mother and grandmother met Cynthia, they thanked God that I had found a spiritual leader and was growing in my faith.

Cynthia's commitment to developing servant leaders brought me into the committed and inspiring leadership of Dave Alexander, the regional minister, and his wife, Anne. I also met Hal and June Doster, Carol Lavery, and Anne Boney, to name some of those early DOC saints in the Christian Church in Georgia. I was chosen to join the New Church Planning team, which included Nettie Craddock, wife of one of the giants of our denomination, Fred Craddock. The Region of Georgia called Hal, Al Widener, and Oscar Haynes to assist Cynthia and the congregation of approximately 70 to 90 members in fundraising to either purchase or build a church home for what Cynthia named Ray of Hope Christian Church. She developed a growth plan that was grounded in evangelism—being witnesses to the love of Jesus in our circle of family, friends, and anyone we met during our daily lives—shopping for groceries, going to the beauty or barber shop—and in the places where we worked and played. She was astute in inviting us to travel with her when she preached locally and sometimes nationally. I grew in my discipleship through visits to Disciples congregations in Georgia and in Memphis. I visited Mississippi Boulevard Christian Church with Cynthia's dear friend, Alvin O. Jackson. At the National Convocation and General Assembly, I observed the faithfulness of leaders of the Black church and the whole church.

I watched, listened, and studied everything Cynthia did. She embodied Christ in a way that was contagious for me and many others. The church grew like wildfire in those first five years. The most profound gift Cynthia gave me was listening for God's voice. She held leadership retreats every year in the fall, away from the church campus. One particular year, she taught us what I came to understand to be the Lectio Divina, where you take a pericope of scripture, read it several times, and listen in silence. She instructed us to place ourselves into the passage and ask God, "What are you saying to me?" She said, sit in silence and listen for God to respond. I took the scripture I had received and my bible and off I went into the woods to find a quiet solitary place to begin my search for God's companionship. I had no burning questions that I needed answered, no search for purpose. I was doing just fine growing in my faith. But I went into the beauty of the woods and rolling hills of the Atlanta suburbs, as an act of obedience to my pastor.

That was the day, I heard God speak to me. I began to cry. I knew it was God because the words that flowed into my consciousness that day were not words that I would have ever imagined for myself. Into my silence and tears God spoke, "Go to seminary." I admit I had a few words of my own for God. More precisely, I had questions for the *Great I Am*. I marvel now at the nerve I had at the time to ask God, "Why?" I am doing everything in the church. I teach Sunday school, new member classes, I am an elder, I am doing everything. Why do I need to go to seminary? As I questioned God, my time of silence was up, and it was time to return to the group. When Cynthia asked if anyone would like to share, I raised my hand. I shared what I heard from God and one of the older elders responded, "Well, duh."

Cynthia responded, "Let's talk about it."

I did not formally schedule a time with her to talk it through, because I didn't want to pursue seminary at the time. Though I did not tell her that. And I certainly didn't want to talk about it with God. I wanted to be married and have two kids, and I was dating someone. I thought he was the one. So , I kept doing what I was doing: working at Georgia State and serving at Ray of Hope with anticipation of the proposal that I just knew was coming by Christmas. Instead of a proposal, I got a broken heart.

Crying through the New Year, I applied to Candler School of Theology, secretly hoping I would not get accepted and that would be the end of it. It did not turn out the way I had hoped. I got accepted! So much for my plan. I went to seminary and loved it, even though I felt like my brain cells were half dead. For the first time in my life, sitting in my first seminary course, I felt whole, satisfied with myself and my relationship with God.

Finding Community

I completed my first year at Candler but did not receive enough scholarship funding for the second year, largely because I was not United Methodist. Cynthia Hale hired me as the Ray's director of Christian Education. It was a good entry into congregational ministry. During this time, I was elected to serve on the Church Extension Board (CEB), now known as Disciples Church Extension. President Hal Watkins came to visit me in person to extend the invitation to serve on the board. While attending a board meeting in Indianapolis, Jim Powell, a staff person, asked me, "What are you doing now?" I shared with him that I had started seminary but had to put it on pause because of the lack of funds. He said, "You know there are Disciples Seminaries where you can get up to 100 percent tuition."

No, I did not know that! Jim's sharing of that knowledge led me to research Disciples seminaries. The one that most appealed to me was Disciples Divinity House (DDH) at the University of Chicago. I planned a campus visit, met Dean Kris Culp, and sat in on a class. I loved it! In 1995, I began the second season of living into God's call to go to seminary. I had no family or friends there, just me in a ready-made community of mostly younger MDiv scholars and PhDs. There I was in a house with 22 other scholars (DOCs and ecumenical students) of varied ages, under one roof. I knew developing friendships as an introvert was not going to be easy. I grounded myself in scripture. There were two in particular that anchored me during the first couple of years.

> For I am with you, and no one is going to attack and harm you, because I have many people in this city. – Acts 18:10 (NRSVUE)

> For surely I know the plans I have for you, says the Lord, plans for your welfare and not for harm, to give you a future with hope. – Jeremiah 29:11(NRSVUE)

These two passages brought me peace even though it still took time for me to make friends. Attending DDH Monday Night Dinners, which included Sherry Hour, a shared meal, lectures, and dialogue, was the key for building friendships and community that nourish me to this day. At Monday Night Dinners, I began to meet Black leaders from Park Manor and Maywood Christian churches who knew my pastor, Cynthia Hale. These were DOC spiritual giants in our denomination, including the National Convocation; people such as Sybel and Harvey Thomas, Delores Highbaugh, Eddie Griffin, Elsie Green, Rev. James Demus, and Revs. Irvin and Betty Green. Irvin was senior pastor at Maywood and a Timothy from Park Manor. I interned under Irvin along with Donald Gillett, who was pursuing his MDiv at McCormick Theological Seminary. Don and Charisse Gillett often gave me rides to Maywood, they were dating at the time. Their son, Jeremy, was around ten years old when I met them. Both Don and Charisse are now serving the church—Don as Kentucky Regional Minister and Charisse as President of Lexington Theological Seminary. And that 10-year-old child is now a playwright, actor, and pastor. Harvey, Sybel and Delores—with Harvey always driving—would come whisk me away for a good meal and conversation. I struggled as a DDH scholar , but these saints kept me from throwing in the towel and going home. They kept me grounded. Pam Jones was a non-DOC resident at the House pursuing her PhD in the History of Christianity. She was closer to me in age and life experience. When a younger resident of House was tripping about something, we would catch each other's eye as a signal of solidarity about the drama we were about to get looped into.

The DDH/University of Chicago Divinity School shaped me with a theology that liberated me to accept that questioning "an all knowing and living God" is faithfulness. I was close to completing my degree when I had a mental break. I was burning the candle at both ends. My friend Pam went to Dean Culp and told her she had not seen me in days. She knew something was wrong. I had shuttered myself in my room and was contemplating quitting the program and going home. I was depressed about too many unfinished papers. I knew I did not have the capacity to finish them by the deadlines. Dean Culp came and knocked on my door. I opened it and she said, "Are you ok?" I said no through uncontrollable tears. She sat down and listened to me. She told me to do two things with her strong Midwestern accent: 1, Start scheduling myself into my calendar on a weekly basis just like I scheduled people, meetings, and papers and 2, Go to the mental health clinic on campus and see the psychiatrist. I did so without delay. The psychiatrist assessed me and prescribed meds and six weeks of counseling. I met with the Dean of the Divinity School and shared what was happening to me. I will never forget what Rick Rosengarten said to me. "There are many students throughout this University who are dealing with depression. I want you to know you always have options." He proceeded to share some options with me. I chose to receive the Master of Theology degree, where I had more than enough hours to graduate. I met with the Illinois/Wisconsin Commission on Ministry, and once again they gave me options.

Having to pivot from my original path in ministry evoked questions: How would I live out my call to ministry? Would it be in the local parish, chaplaincy, regional, general church, or a non-profit? Was I ready after hitting the wall mentally? What were my options? I had interned with Norma Ellington-Twitty at the National Benevolent Association on a project with children. I had experience in Christian education and leader development at Ray of Hope. But what was God calling me to with the education of the last three years? Dean Culp recommended I do an independent study with Dr. Stephanie Paulsell. She immersed me in a course on Spirituality and Spiritual Practices. I read and dialogued with her on Teresa of Avila, Abraham Joshua Heschel, Simone Weil, Dorothy Bass, and others. She placed one penetrating question before me, "Joan, do you feel called to be on the journey with people day in and day out? Or do you want to be in and out of people's lives as a regional or general church leader?" I knew I wanted to be on the journey with people every day. Dr. Paulsell had asked me the right question.

In my last year of divinity school, I found love in the person of Oscar Haynes, one of the denomination's most faithful servants and the best revelation of Jesus I had the privilege of living life with for more than sixteen years. Remember, he was a part of the Capital Campaign Team that guided Cynthia Hale and Ray of Hope in raising funds to purchase our first church home. He was my senior by thirty-eight years! Once again, it was not the narrative I had intended. I sought discernment with companions, my best girlfriend, and my wise Mom. But had I not taken the matter to God, I might have missed the blessing of deep love and companionship. This leadership journey of mine has come with costs, upheaval, lost of friends—and lots of uncertainty. For someone who had worked her whole life to create a path that was certain and comfortable, I found myself living in uncertainty but seeking the heart of God for myself. It is hard living on the "growing edge". But it is marvelous growing into who God created me to be: God's beloved.

Wisdom for the Journey

There is wisdom in this journey. I invite you to consider these pearls from my life.

1. God calls us to our places of preparation and discernment. In those places, God will also surround you with a community. Embrace that community and give them permission to embrace you.
2. Give attention to your own well-being and seek support when you need it.
3. Root yourself in spiritual practices. Prayer, meditation, nature, and fasting among other practices will anchor your faith and your ministry.
4. Be open to deep love and companionship at any age.

A Final Word

The call to lead God's people in the many places where God needs you is a journey of discernment, travel, and action. It is a journey of companionship, friendships, hardships, doubts, tears, and tremendous joy. I again invite you to discern the pearls from my journey and excavate your journey to offer wisdom to the next generation of leaders.

— ***Rev. Joan Bell-Haynes*** *is the former regional minister of the Christian Church in the Central Rocky Mountain Region and the Christian Church in Georgia. She was the first woman and African American to serve in the position in the Central Rocky Mountain Region and the second to serve in the role in the Georgia region.*

I Am A Girl

I Stepped Out Because I Believed

Rev. Dr. Delesslyn A. Kennebrew

And straightway Jesus constrained his disciples to get into a ship, and to go before him unto the other side, while he sent the multitudes away. And when he had sent the multitudes away, he went up into a mountain apart to pray: and when the evening was come, he was there alone. But the ship was now in the midst of the sea, tossed with waves: for the wind was contrary. And in the fourth watch of the night Jesus went unto them, walking on the sea. And when the disciples saw him walking on the sea, they were troubled, saying, It is a spirit; and they cried out for fear. But straightway Jesus spake unto them, saying, Be of good cheer; it is I; be not afraid. And Peter answered him and said, Lord, if it be thou, bid me come unto thee on the water. And he said, Come. And when Peter was come down out of the ship, he walked on the water, to go to Jesus. But when he saw the wind boisterous, he was afraid; and beginning to sink, he cried, saying, Lord, save me. And immediately Jesus stretched forth his hand, and caught him, and said unto him, O thou of little faith, wherefore didst thou doubt? And when they were come into the ship, the wind ceased. Then they that were in the ship came and worshipped him, saying, Of a truth thou art the Son of God. (Matthew 14:22-33), (KJV)

I Am a Girl

I grew up in church.
I am a preacher's kid.
I am a girl.
I learned the books of the Bible.
I memorized passages of scripture in the Bible.
I fell in love with the God of the Bible.

I am a girl.
I believed in God.
I trusted God the Son as my Savior.
And I relied on the guidance, comfort, and teaching of the Holy Spirit.
I am a girl.

I accepted and acknowledged the Lord as my Savior when I was 9 years old on the third Sunday of January 1987. I was baptized by my father, Bishop Vernon Kennebrew, and my late godfather, Deacon Gary Brumfield, one month later in a white baptismal gown and cap sewn by my late grandmother, Sister Mary Helen Kennebrew. At 9, I did not have a complete understanding of the continual process of salvation and sanctification. I just knew that I had to be a good girl, a good church girl.

I was taught that I could do ALL things through Christ who gives me strength (Philippians 4:13). And I believed it.

I was taught that in Christ, there is neither Jew nor Greek, there is neither bond nor free, there is neither male nor female: for ye are all one in Christ Jesus (Galatians 3:28). And I believed it.

I was taught that before God formed me in my mother's womb, God knew me, and before I came out of my mother's womb, God sanctified me and called me, and God had already set me aside to do God's work in the world (Jeremiah 1:5). And I believed it.

I believed it all.

And I am a girl.

I have been going to church since I was in my mother's womb. I cannot recall a period in my life where church attendance, ministry participation, and my faith were not a part of the wonderings and wanderings of my daily life. This is not to say that I have been saved my entire life, but it is to say that I have had an awareness of God for as long as I can remember. And I am a girl.

Matthew 14 is one of my favorite passages of scripture. Peter steps out of the boat and walks on water. Just before he does so, he says, "Lord, if it's you, order me to come to you on the water."

And Jesus said, "Come."

Then Peter got out of the boat and was walking on the water toward Jesus (Matthew 14:28-29, CEB). This holy moment best describes my life and ministry. I am always looking for opportunities to trust God to step out of the boat and to walk on water by faith.

Then I *experienced* Matthew 14. My chapter lasted longer than the minute it takes for anyone to read that passage. I, like the disciples, was going along in the safety of the boat that had been built by my family, friends, church members, and Sunday School teachers. They and so many others loved me, poured into me, and sacrificed for me. I was riding along in the safety of the boat that been created by their prayers and doctrines, discipline, and truth.

But then the storm of my life—brought about by the clash of my gender and my tradition —was released into the atmosphere as I pursued my destiny. I struggled with the shift of the direction of this call from the Lord, who was now calling me to step out of that boat.

But Lord, I am a girl.

Lord, I am a girl.

Walking on Water

For years, as far back as my teenage years, I remember telling the Lord, "Lord, I am a girl." The Lord was calling and I could see glimpses of the Lord walking on the water, but this storm was raging in my body, spirit, church, and family. It was my desire and destiny to obey.

Lord, I know you understand the situation I am in. I will say YES, but let me stay in the boat, because if I say YES without parameters, without limits, without boundaries, I will have to get out of the boat and I will have to walk on water. Lord, I don't know any girls in my life who have done that. I don't have anyone in my life who will support that. Lord, please let me say YES but inside the familiarity and comfort of this boat.

For many years, the Lord allowed me to stay in the boat, mercifully withholding his wrath, because I kept telling Him that I am a girl.

Then in 2002, I entered my final year of law school. And the Lord appeared again on the water and told me that in this next year, "You will have a decision to make. Your decision will be to either follow me or stay in the boat."

In the fall of 2003, and for the entire first year of seminary, I wrestled because I knew what it cost for me to step out of the boat. But I also knew what it would cost for me to stay in the boat. And in my heart of hearts, I was willing to risk everything to be obedient to what I knew the Lord was calling me to do.

The issue for the Lord was never about my gender. The issue, the call was always about my obedience to all of the scripture I said I believed.

In the summer of 2004, I decided that I did not want to risk being disobedient to the One who knew I was girl when He called me. So, I stepped out of the boat, and I have been walking on water ever since the Lord gave me the final call to COME.

Friends, I do not know what your boat looks like. I do not know how long you have been wrestling within yourself to stay in the boat. I do not know how many excuses you have made to keep the boat exactly where it is. I do not know anything about your boat. All I know is that ever since I stepped out of mine, I have walked on water and in true FREEDOM as God has used me to live out the call that God placed on my life.

When I stepped out, the Lord told me, "Do not argue about your call. I will defend you." The Lord told me, "You do not have to prove to anyone that you are called. I will cover you." The Lord instructed me to: JUST LIVE IT. And God will handle the rest.

It is out of my obedience that God chooses to use this vessel, who happens to be in a girl's body, to proclaim the glorious Gospel of the Lord Jesus Christ.

I can only imagine the thoughts of Peter as he sat in that boat wrestling within himself while in the midst of this storm. Jesus had sent them ahead and into a turbulent time. A few chapters earlier, Jesus was with them in the boat when the storm arose. He was sleep, but He was there. But now, He was not physically with them in this boat. Yet Jesus had to know that a storm was on the way. I believe that Jesus also knew it was time to put what the disciples said they believed to the test.

So, Peter is in the boat and is probably experiencing a tinge of fear as he sits with his friends. "And in the fourth watch of the night—between 3 a.m. and 6 a.m. —Jesus went unto them, walking on the sea. And when the disciples saw him walking on the sea, they were troubled, saying, "It is a spirit; and they cried out for fear." But straightway Jesus spake unto them—as He continues to speak unto me and unto you in whatever storm you may find yourself in—saying, "Be of good cheer; it is I; be not afraid."

Then Peter takes him at his word. Peter believed the Son of God. Peter prays, "Lord, if it be you, bid me to come."

I can only imagine the likely insults and shaming the other disciples shouted at him—the side eyes, the backbiting, the doubting, the accusatory tones, and the degrading remarks simply because he/I wanted to follow Jesus. He/I wanted to experience Jesus in a way that he/I had never experienced Jesus before.

In those days, there was an ancient belief that there were monsters in the sea, and seeing this shadowy figure moving toward them, the disciples thought surely that could not be Jesus. Jesus does not look like that. Jesus does not sound like that. Jesus would not use that. I know Jesus. We know Jesus and that ain't Him…except it was.

It was Jesus doing the unexpected, unpredictable, the unprecedented in the middle of a storm. It was Jesus doing what they had never seen or heard of before. It was Jesus moving in their lives in a different kind of way. It was JESUS. And Peter was the only one who believed.

I believed God and I, much like Peter, prayed:

> Lord, if it be you.
> I hear what people are saying…but Lord, if it be you…
> I cannot tell in the midst of this storm of my life—in my family—
> on my job…but Lord, if it be you…

I am a girl. I am just a fisherman. I am just this. I am just that. I don't have this. I don't have that. And I usually stay in the boat. But I don't want to miss this opportunity to experience the miraculous in my life. So, Lord, if it be you, bid me to come. Lord, invite me to do something different. Lord, invite me to be a light in this dark world. Lord, invite me to be a peacemaker and a justice worker. Lord, invite me to do the greater works that you have promised we would do. Lord, invite me to experience FREEDOM in you.

Lord, if it be you, bid me to come.

And the Lord said: COME…

And when Peter came down out of the ship, he walked on the water, to go to Jesus.

In August 2004, I stepped all the way out of the boat when I preached my first sermon. I have been walking in FREEDOM and walking on water ever since.

> And I am still a girl.
> But I only stepped out because I believed.
> YES!

I admit it has not been easy. I have experienced loneliness, and there were times when I second, third, and fourth guessed myself. And like Peter, I have had to ask the Lord to save me when I felt like I was drowning due to my fear of staying outside the boat, drowning due to the rejection I have experienced because I stepped outside of the boat, and drowning due to the loneliness while in the company of those I love. I have cried out to the Lord: *Lord, Save Me!*

Seminary was a formative and transformative time for my spiritual journey, particularly as it relates to answering God's call to proclaim the Gospel. I grew up in a denomination that does not license or ordain women to preach. So, when I made the decision to make my call public at the church I was attending, my family did not celebrate with me, and the church of my birth thought I was lost. I felt so alone. But I knew what the Lord had called me to do. In this girl body, I had to say, Yes, Lord!

My yes did not come without critique, rejection, or whispers behind my back and in front of my face. My yes cost me years of strained relationships with the people I loved the most. My yes meant I had to leave the denomination of my birth and baptism. My yes meant no family was at my licensing or ordination, except for one first cousin.

My yes also meant that I have lived out my call with no regret of saying yes in the first place. The Lord has been extremely faithful to make room for my gifts to teach, preach, administrate, innovate, lead, and serve. The Lord has brought me into safe spaces that have affirmed God's call and my obedience to it.

Wisdom For the Next Generation

Friends, if you do decide to heed the Lord's call or command in your life to step out of the boat, I want you to know that if you just keep your eyes on Jesus once you step out of the boat—and THIS IS MY TESTIMONY—you will learn and experience:

1. You will go where no one in your life has gone before, but in God you will have the kind of FREEDOM that only faith can handle and a peace that surpasses all understanding.
2. Your faith will lead you to walk further away from the boat because you will have to say yes every single day.
3. Your walk will be a witness to those inside of any boat that God really is able to do exceeding abundantly above all you could ever ask, think, or believe. You become what is possible if *they* would only believe.

4. You do not have to stay mad at them for staying in the boat or not supporting your choice to step out of the boat.

When you make the decision to answer the Lord's call in your life to COME, please know that the Lord has already prepared a way for you. You may not know every place you will go along your journey, but you will know at least the one next step in the right direction. This path will lead you to where no one in your life has gone simply because they made the decision, for whatever reason, not to accept the Lord's invitation to them. I cannot explain the profound freedom of spirit and peace of mind that will grow inside of you every time you take one step in the direction of the Lord's call. Friend, just step out and keep walking!

When Peter stepped out of the boat, he was stepping away from what was comfortable and who was familiar. I know this can be hard. I have cried many tears and had many restless nights, because I wanted others to see the vision I saw and to celebrate this good thing that God was doing. But friends, many will not see what you see, and many will not rejoice when you rejoice. You have to get ok with that. When you tell the Lord yes, you are also saying no to the boundaries, boxes, and preconceived notions that others have preset for you. They will not understand. They will not like it. They will tell you that they think you have got it all wrong. But when the Lord invites you to come, say yes again and again and again anyway.

I stepped out because I believed. I believed what I had been taught, and I believed I was included in every promise. There are so many who will do their very best to narrow the parameters around who is included in the God story as it is lived out today. I am so grateful they are not God. I am so grateful that all we have to do is believe and accept God's never-ending invitation to be present with God and to serve others as God leads. Let your witness be an announcement to others that God uses girls too, and young people too, and laypeople too, and any other group that has been marginalized, left out, looked over, or laid aside too. Open your mind when you say yes, Lord, to the endless possibilities that might become available to you for the glory of God! Friend, let God blow your mind and keep walking!

Pray for those who stay in the boat, recognizing that their choice to limit their faith to the confines of whatever boat they find themselves in is between them and the Lord. It is not your battle to fight. Some might even try to step out but will not stay out long enough to get to the other side. In this text, the Lord did help Peter get back into the boat that he had stepped out of, but I believe that because of his fear, Peter missed the opportunity to walk on water all the way to the other side. We do not have another biblical account of Peter trying again. However, I want to believe that the Lord will continue to extend an invitation and provide spaces for you to walk on water. Friend, keep your eyes on Jesus and keep on walking!

A Final Word

In your quiet time, I invite you to reflect on these three questions:

1. What are the barriers, beliefs, or fears that keep you in the boats of your life?
2. How has the Lord invited you to walk on water in your life lately?
3. Why have you accepted or rejected the invitation of the Lord?

In your quiet time, I invite you to consider the fruit that will emerge from your reflections. Write them down. Pray over them. Act on them. "Whatever you do, whether in speech or action, do it all in the name of the Lord Jesus and give thanks to God the Father through him." (Colossians 3:17, CEB)

— ***Rev. Dr. Delesslyn A. Kennebrew****, J.D., MDiv., is the first African American woman to serve as the settled Administrative Secretary of the National Convocation and Associate General Minister of the Christian Church (Disciples of Christ).*

Leadership
Finding My Voice and My Way

Charisse L. Gillett

> Do not be conformed to this world, but be transformed by the renewing of your mind, so that you may discern what is the will of God—what is good, acceptable, and perfect. (Romans 12:2, NRSV)

I realized as I wrote this essay that I have been thinking about my experiences in leadership for a long time and writing about them a little here and a little there. In my article, *What Charisse Saw: Reflections on the Intersection of Race and Gender—Narrative and Knowing* (2020), I expounded on my observations of power and the ability to cultivate and exercise power from a minority position. In my essay, *Reflections on Leadership in an Era of COVID-19 and in the Midst of a Reckoning on Racial Injustice (2021)*, I looked back on my call to the presidency of Lexington Theological Seminary, sharing thoughts on operating during institutional crisis, the global COVID-19 pandemic, and the deaths of Brianna Taylor and George Floyd. Both essays tell a fraction of the story. In my memoir, *That Little Girl: Memories, Challenges and Reflections on Black Girl Dreams (2025)*, I shared some of my earliest memories of being nurtured, loved, and prayed into the person I am today. In this essay, I share specific reflections on leadership and the reception my leadership has received in different venues. I hope to reveal the essence of my experience as a window into my journey. The epilogue to *That Little Girl* hints at the rest of the story. This essay is a contribution to that story.

While reading bell hooks' Y*earning, Race, Gender, and Cultural Politics,* I fell in love with the word "drysolong" (p.40). The word is a combination of the words *dry*, *so*, and *long*. The three words are smooshed together to create something new. Seeing the word drysolong in print and saying it aloud spoke to me about the ways in which we tend to discuss important topics without saying much. Often for the sake of protocol or for the good of order, words are used to pretty up and cover over the pain and discord of professional and organizational challenges. These words are used in ways that are not helpful to solutions and progress. Our conversations are careful, curated, and sub rosa. They have been drysolong of helpful truths that the necessary healing, thriving, and flourishing for the upbuilding of God's kin-dom is stymied and delayed. Indeed, my own healing, thriving, and flourishing was stymied by such conversations. I share all of this to be a resource for the next generation of African American women leaders, so I speak in my own voice and give witness to another chapter in the rest of my story. I hope my words will be received as water to seeds of truth and hope.

Disrespect is Cumulative

Three recent experiences caused me to think about the cumulative impact of being overlooked. Indeed, I recounted the three incidents to a group of colleagues, concluding with the statement, "The disrespect is cumulative." As I shared the stories, I noticed that months later I was still irritated. The first incident related to the publication of an article. I, along with a group of leaders, volunteered to serve as respondents. The group met to discuss an approach to the article to which we were responding. The process took about a year. Finally, after a year, I received the email notifying contributors that the publication was online and available, along with the link to the finished product. I eagerly clicked on the link. I wanted to read the work of my colleagues and their responses to the foundational article. I liked the design of the publication. It used images of the authors near their byline and the title of their article. I clicked through the resource and found my article and then went back to the table of contents. I clicked through the resource again and I noticed that my picture was missing. Trying to make sense of it, I reasoned that only a handful of authors would be featured; therefore, only a handful of pictures were needed. I reviewed the resource and confirmed that my image was the only one missing from the introduction next to my article.

The second incident was related to the edits I recommended for a soon-to-be-published book. I was given a deadline of 24 to 48 hours to respond, which I did. I sent the author a note with four to five edits but indicated two edits were non-negotiable. One edit addressed a description of organizational partners that invited misunderstanding, and the other edit addressed language that was culturally tone-deaf. I sent an email to the author along with an explanation about the edits, and less than five minutes later I received a curt email saying, *"It's too late for that."*

The third incident occurred during the last moments of a two-day meeting. The president of the organization began to thank those rotating off the advisory board for their commitment and service. To the people rotating off the board, kind and heartfelt words of gratitude were offered and small tokens of appreciation were given. Then, realizing there were not enough gifts for everyone, the president said, "Oh, thank you Charisse. We will get something to you later." Almost immediately, the editor of the journal, the person for whom I was reviewing the book, and the president of the organization understood that what transpired was not reflective of our professional relationship or my visible commitment and contributions to the organizations and projects represented in these vignettes. I received apologies, explanations, and expressions of regret, which I accepted. These moments were an unwelcome reminder that I began my journey as the president of Lexington Theological Seminary being undermined and dismissed publicly by a member of the community. These real-life incidents reminded me, as I said to my friends and colleagues, that "the disrespect is cumulative."

For me, it is not that one thing happened. It is that after decades of leadership across multiple venues, such things continue to happen. Each time this happens, I have an internal physical reaction that amounts to rage…yes, you did not misread the word. It is rage. It is rage because I am deeply aware that I have made transformative contributions to the places where I show up and my deep commitment to the activities, events, and committees *requires sacrifice.* The rage deepens when those involved are women, and it is even more painful when women of color are involved, as was the case in at least one of these incidents. The issue is also most disturbing and confounding when I am at the center of this kind of situation for other women, and in particular women of color. In other words, I, too, have been the source of someone's discomfort and have precipitated someone else's rage.

On this journey, I need manna to sustain my capacity for leadership, stay involved, remain at the table, and respond with grace when my efforts are marginalized. For those of us leading and those aspiring to lead, it is critical to recognize God's daily provision that permits us to remain whole and encouraged on the journey.

Resilient Faith

The God, who knows me best and the one to whom I pray and give thanks has always been in my life. Not in the sense that I grew up in a home of weekly church attendance; rather in the sense that faith, prayer, and thanksgiving were acts of daily living. My parents, Vivian Brown and Clayton Brown, were simply too exhausted after working two jobs and taking care of seven children Monday through Saturday to then spend all day in church on Sunday. We went to church as it was part of our lives, but it was not the choir practice on Tuesday and Thursday, Bible Study on Wednesday, deacon meeting on Thursday, and church outing on Saturday kind of church attendance. The God I experienced in my parents' home was profusely thanked for food, safety, employment, a house with enough rooms for a family of nine, and educational opportunities. This God was given thanks for the clothes on our backs, the shoes on our feet, the car to drive to work, especially during Chicago winters, and a little extra money to put up for Christmas and the inevitable rainy day. This God was living in the heart of our existence, and my parents gave thanks for the practical things that enriched their lives and those of their children. The choir practice, Bible study, deacon meeting, sunup-to-sundown on Sunday God was the God I witnessed in the summer when I visited my paternal family in southern Indiana. This is the God my aunt, uncle, and Granny sent home to Chicago with me. Aunt Armetta and Uncle Stephen told me often, "I prayed and asked God to protect you all in Chicago. It is a dangerous place. I prayed for God's protection for you kids, your mother, and Brother." (Although his name was Clayton, my dad's siblings called him "Brother.") My grandmother made sure I learned to pray for myself. "Risse, make sure you say your prayers," Granny said. "Make sure you talk to God. Make sure you know Jesus. Make sure you thank God." My parents, aunt, uncle, and Granny modeled for me a can-do, will-do, must-do, never-give-up faith.

It is this faith that I took and made my own. This is the faith that travelled with me into crooked rooms and pulpits that would have me contort my very being while trying to respond faithfully to the work God called me to do. In *Sister Citizens: For Colored Girls Who've Considered Politics When Being Strong Isn't Enough,* Melissa Harris Perry recounts the post-World War II cognitive psychology research that describes how subjects tilt themselves in crooked rooms in crooked chairs and perceive themselves to be upright in relationship to distorted spaces. In *Shifting: The Double Lives of Black Women in American*, Charisse Jones and Kumea Shorter-Gooden report on the ways in which Black women accommodate, deflect, and respond to stereotypes, perceptions, and the needs of others by shifting their voice, language, and perspectives. Early in my leadership, it wasn't clear to me that the spaces I entered were crooked and that I would need to shift to be heard and seen. To be clear, showing up in spaces that present as welcoming but only welcome if one distorts oneself to be seen and heard is the context. Crooked rooms and pulpits and shifting are about the subjugation of self to be heard and seen, not about the necessary growth to become an effective leader. These two concepts are not the same, and I was not prepared for this reality. Simply put, I believed those who encouraged me to be bold and speak up. I believed the people who encouraged my intellect, courage, and abilities. I believed the social and cultural messages that I could be anything I wanted to be if I was prepared, worked hard enough, and made the necessary sacrifices. I missed the sub rosa messaging that as a Black woman, my options were limited. It was not until I heard my ideas reframed and presented by others, not until my observations were greeted with polite acknowledgment, only to be embraced when spoken word-for-word by someone else, days later or in the same meeting—only then did I realize, *They want me to show up, but not speak up*. Coming to terms with this was frustrating and painful. I kept showing up and when I did, I would ask God in irritation and anger, "Why am I here? What should I take from this horrible experience?"

And then I would call my CPA/MBA sister, Carla, and talk for hours about the similarities between her experiences in business and mine in church and higher education. I would talk with my maternal aunt, Lillian Davis, a woman who broke barriers as a civic leader in Indianapolis. My sister and I would debrief and help each other strategize for the next meeting. My aunt would listen and help me interpret my emotions and the reality of the meetings from the perspective of a seasoned leader and Black woman who had in her own time faced challenges. Sometimes I would describe to them my decision to truncate answers or pretty-up my responses with the notion that I needed to live to fight another day. I am grateful neither of them denied my experience, tried to explain it away, or judged me for sometimes taking the path of least resistance. Sometimes it was simply too much to sit at tables that required me to justify my existence, as if my credentials, experience, title, savvy, and preparation were not enough. Sometimes it was too much to watch others take credit for my hard work and ideas. Sometimes I would walk out of meetings. Sometimes I disappeared while I was present. Sometimes in the moment, I fought the good fight. Carla, Aunt Lillian, and God were my conversation partners. They did not judge.

In my long season of maturing and learning, I reached for the God my parents showed me—the one who was always there, the God my Granny told me to talk with and to whom I prayed. I cultivated a prayer life and a faith that invited conversation and authenticity. I leaned into this prayer life when it looked like I would give in to feelings of resentment from living in religious and professional spaces that wanted my presence, but not my giftedness. I developed as a mature leader, giving attention to my intellect, spirit, and soul. I developed a resilient faith that strengthened me at every turn. On this journey I am reminded by the scripture from Romans 12:2, "Do not be conformed to this world, but be transformed by the renewing of your mind, so that you may discern what is the will of God—what is good, acceptable, and perfect." In maturing I learned not to conform or shift in spaces and in crooked rooms and crooked pulpits.

To paraphrase Ms. Celie from *The Color Purple*, "I am Black. I am a woman. I did not go to your school. I do not know your tribe. But thanks be to God! I am here!" Each time I enter a room, sit at a table, or join a conversation, each time I show up I am determined to offer my gifts and say to myself, "Whatever happens, I will not conform. I will not be ignored. I will be prepared. I AM HERE."

Leadership Formation

I will not conform. I will be prepared. These are bold statements and strong internal mantras for an African American woman with aspirations. It was not enough for me to know that I wanted to lead. I needed significant opportunities to lead and be seen as a leader. In the academy, such opportunities took the form of serving on committees, chairing task forces, volunteering for assignments, and being active in my professional associations. In the church, such opportunities presented themselves by serving on regional and national boards and volunteering for time-limited projects. I said "yes" to every opportunity to gain experience about leadership, learn about myself, and to lead. When Dick Hamn, the General Minister and President of the Christian Church (Disciples of Christ) called and asked me to allow my name to go forth as moderator of the Christian Church, I said yes. I served as moderator from 2003–2005. According to the Design of the Christian Church, the moderator conducts the business of the church, leads the church in spiritual and business matters, and presides at the General Assembly. The culminating experience was presiding at the General Assembly of the Christian Church in Portland, Oregon. It was an extraordinary opportunity to serve the church, and I witnessed the church at its best and most troubling. I also witnessed a part of history as the first woman was elected General Minister and President. This happened during my term as moderator, so I was honored to be a part of this special moment.

When John Foulkes called me in 2003 to ask me to serve as secretary of the National Convocation, I said yes. When my mentor in 2004 advised me to participate in a series of leadership skills testing, I knew enough to know I needed a solid leadership assessment of my skills to grow as a leader, and so I said yes. In 2007, I said yes to the Kaleidoscope Leadership Institute for Women in Higher Education, and in 2009, I said yes to the first class of the Foundations of Christian Leadership program in collaboration with the Center for Creative Leadership and Leadership Education at Duke Divinity (funded by

Lilly Endowment Inc.). I said yes to all of it as a means of preparing for a role as a leader in an organization that would someday allow me to bring together my values of family, faith, and education. These experiences gave me insights into collaborating with people of influence, power, privilege, ambition, and human flaws. Sadly, in the church and academy I was equally inspired by the brilliance and disappointed by the smallness of God's people.

Formation as a leader required that I intentionally engage in situations that would make me uncomfortable and challenge my ability to articulate a counter narrative. Learning to adapt with integrity strengthened my capacity and vision for my own leadership. My leadership formation is ongoing and requires relationships with honest mentors, thoughtful and culturally competent executive coaches, attendance at leadership symposiums, and perfecting a graceful way to tell the truth. The bottom line is: I pay attention to my own growth and maturity as a leader.

Wisdom for the Next Generation

I would like to think that African American women who aspire to executive leadership will not encounter crooked rooms and pulpits and will not have the experience of shifting to be seen and heard. The truth is that as long as there are systems that value and privilege certain kinds of people and leadership styles, African American women will have these experiences. The disrespect is cumulative. For me, the manna on the journey has been a resilient faith. My family nurtured in me, by their examples, a God that showed up in our lives. My faith has a God that shows up in ways that have sustained me when the promotion went to a coworker, when confidences were betrayed, when the paycheck did not fit my responsibilities, and when it seemed as if I was professionally stuck. It is my faith that kept me moving forward with a yes when there was no evidence I should hang on to my dreams. My wisdom for the next generation is to cultivate a resilient faith. Cultivate spiritual habits, practices, and a community that allows you to trust in the things you cannot see but are most certainly hoping for.

I said yes to opportunities that allowed me to deepen my leaderships skills. I was not always the one leading, but the experience of being at the table for discussions with people committed to the same issues gave me much-needed perspective. It was only in community that I could observe leaders bring people together to create space for collaboration and thoughtful solutions. It was only in these venues that I could witness the sincere work of the community derailed by others equally committed to their ideas. My wisdom for the next generation is to say yes to opportunities, engage those with whom you disagree and stay at the table.

I am committed to my growth as a leader. I seek mentors, attend leadership conferences, and accept helpful critique to expand my capacities as a leader. I deal as forthrightly as I can with my own shortcomings as a leader. My wisdom for the next generation is to pay attention to your growth as a leadership. Leaders don't always get it right, but we owe it to ourselves and the institutions we serve to mature and do our best to make new mistakes.

A Final Word

May Sarton's poem *Now I Become Myself* is a favorite of mine. The first four lines resonate with me:

> Now I become myself. It's taken
>
> Time, many years and places,
>
> I have been dissolved and shaken,
>
> Worn other people's faces...

As you grow and become you, do not be ashamed or afraid that you will try on other people's faces, mannerisms, voice, and cadence. Do not run away from the fact that you will be dissolved and shaken when you enter this realm of leadership. It will happen. In the midst of it all, look for yourself, your rage, your voice, your style, and your giftedness. Do not become drysolong. Look for the seeds planted and watered by your faith, in your soul.

Be who God intends you to be. Learn, Grow, and Flourish.

— ***Rev. Dr. Charisse L. Gillett*** *is the first woman and first African American to serve as president of Lexington Theological Seminary. She is the longest-serving president in the Seminary's modern history.*

References

bell, h. (2015). *Yearning: Race, Gender and Cultural Politics.* Routledge.

Harris-Perry, M. V. (2011). *Sister Citizen: Shame, Stereotypes, and Black Women in America For Colored Girls Who've Consider Politics When Being Strong Isn't Enough.* Yale University Press.

Jones, C. and Gooden-Shorter, K. (2003). *Shifting the Double Lives of Black Women in America.* Harper Collins.

Sarton. M. (1993). Now I Become Myself. from ***Collected Poems 1930 – 1993*** by May Sarton © W.W. Norton, 1993

Vocational Leadership

The Convergence of Formation and Personal Transformation

Bishop Valerie Melvin

It all started on my front porch. My first memory of leadership began somewhere between 1968 and 1969, on a small front porch with twelve baby dolls lined up in a perfect row—the original Melvin Apostles. I was their teacher, and they were my students—the most obedient class I have ever had. I was a little girl, but something in me delighted in sharing what was inside me: an emerging ability to see, name, and excavate the gifts and talents in others, even if my others were made of plastic and cloth.

I did not have language to define leadership, but I recognized the feeling of holiness. Those porch moments felt strangely like worship. On Sundays, I would sit in the church sanctuary and quietly pack away pieces of the liturgy: the music that stirred my soul, the Scriptures read with reverence, the importance of memorizing sacred texts, and yes, life-changing sermons. During the week, I carried those treasures back to the front porch, reenacting them with my dolls. Looking back, I realized my soul was rehearsing its calling.

Fast-forwarding to 1978, I was seated on a football field during my high school graduation, listening to the commencement speaker. Somewhere amid the predictable words of encouragement and congratulations, I heard another voice—clear, purposeful, and utterly unexpected: *Teach my people, because ignorance abounds.* I turned to see who had spoken, but no one near me matched the voice I heard. The only voice coming through the microphone belonged to the speaker on the platform. That question—*Who spoke to me?*—lingered for years. As I matured in faith, I came to understand that it was the Holy Spirit who had spoken, and the vague stirrings from my childhood porch began to solidify into a call: I was being summoned into the teaching ministry.

It is no accident that I spent more than twenty years as a public school music teacher, pouring my energy, creativity, and care into students from kindergarten through twelfth grade and later into adults in community college job readiness classes. Within the education arena, I had a key realization: I loved leading, but not alone. I cherished the idea of working with others, believing that more ideas always lead to better concepts. Therefore, when opportunities like Lead Teacher, School Event Coordinator, Long Range Planning chairperson, and County Music Festival Co-chairperson arose, I readily accepted them. Our collaborative work yielded tangible results, leading to accolades and culminating in being honored as my school's Teacher of the Year twice. My work was positively impacting the community, and I felt profoundly fulfilled. For a long time, I believed this professional success represented the full measure of God's call. I was teaching God's people, shaping minds and hearts, and preparing future citizens. *This must be the call—what God wants me to do,* I told myself. And it was—in part.

The Unforgettable Voice

Calling, in its uncanny nature, unfolds in layers. God's voice does not cease after a single summons. Throughout the Christian journey, we are called from one dimension of selfless service to the next, often stretched beyond what we imagined possible. Every new location, role, and relationship invited me deeper into service, and with each transition, I felt a parallel, undeniable need to reinvest in my original nature, character, and personhood. I did not always honor this need fully. There were seasons when I neglected self-formation, which detrimentally affected my capacity to love beyond myself, relinquish control, or release a role when the time came. Those lessons were hard-earned, but they became crucial parts of my leadership story. The loving wisdom of my family, several mentors, accountability partners, and professional colleagues consistently challenged me to push through and reach my potential.

In the classroom, I learned more about human value and worth than I could ever capture in a single volume. My students arrived from every conceivable walk of life—some raw, some polished; some happy, some melancholy; some extroverted and fearless, others introverted and cautious. Their personalities had been shaped by family and cultural dynamics and by the villages that raised them—or, in some cases, failed to. Over the years, I came to understand village as any group of people who provide a sense of worth, value, and communal respect.

My life became immersed in these varied villages, and my perspective on community, identity, and resilience broadened in ways I had never anticipated. I thought, *Surely this is my zenith. This is the fulfillment of my call.*

From instructing baby dolls to excavating the real-life gifts of people of all ages, my path had been clear. What else could be expected? Yet, just when I believed my calling was complete, the Holy Spirit spoke again, with the same clear, unmistakable words I first heard on that football field, *Teach my people, because ignorance abounds.* This time, I recognized the voice immediately. Hearing it anew, however, forced me to wrestle with a difficult truth: I had not reached the end of my vocation; I had reached a turning point. The teaching I understood was expanding into something more—something that would draw me into the life of the church in ways that demanded deeper faith, higher risk, and a more intentional surrender. A true calling is not a seasonal project with a completion checklist. Calling is, and always will be, a surrendered, lifelong purpose of making a difference, evolving through every season of our lives, spilling Christ's light and love into every space of darkness.

Smoothing the Seams of Transition

As I discerned this next phase, I did not walk alone. I sat at the feet of several mentors who helped to ground my understanding of ministry and leadership in reality, not fantasy.

Rev. Evelyn Gettis Lee of Sure Foundation Institute reminded me that I did not need to preach like a man or lead like one to be effective. I could stand fully and unapologetically in the woman God created, exuding femininity, and still make a profound difference in my generation. Her counsel helped free me from subconscious pressure to mimic models of leadership that did not reflect my identity or experience.

Rev. Bishop William Barber II of the Poor People's Campaign provided a crucial corrective to my academic pursuits, emphasizing that degrees alone would never justify my calling. He pressed me to understand that the extensive theological knowledge gained from my two degrees at Duke Divinity would be meaningless unless I poured that learning into the praxis of local church ministry and community engagement. Bishop Barber intentionally engaged me in hands-on work—social justice initiatives, preaching moments, teaching venues, and intense one-on-one conversations. This experience ignited a fire within me, compelling me to learn how to translate complex divinity school language into clear, accessible speech for any audience. Bishop Barber recognized my intellectual capability, and the specific challenge of framing the theological language I had only recently encountered. Citing the famous United Negro College Fund slogan, "A mind is a terrible thing to waste," he encouraged me not just to use my mental abilities for personal growth but for the fulfillment of purpose. Under his guidance, I fully grasped that a theological mind unused in service to humanity is, precisely, a terrible waste.

Bishop T. Garrett Benjamin, a spiritual mentor and episcopal father, helped me navigate the delicate distinction between form and function in ministry. He taught me that titles, structures, methods, and outward manifestations are merely the containers of ministry, never its essence. The true function is the product: my service to God and others. "A title never makes the person," Bishop Benjamin would say. "It is always the Spirit's work through you that matters." He then admonished me that answering these calls—as the first female Bishop emanating from the Church of Christ and the first woman and person of color to serve as Regional Minister for the Christian Church in North Carolina—a state fraught with racial unrest and patriarchal inequities—would cost me something, perhaps many things, within both churches. This forced me to face the critical questions: *Am I willing to serve, even when I am afraid? Have I counted up the cost of being a pioneer? Do I know what it means to wade in blood for righteousness' sake?*

In addition, time allowed many precious pilgrims—spiritual guides and companions—to walk with me for a season. Though too numerous to name, their coaching was instrumental in my development. They helped me achieve the following:

Discerning and deepening my relationship with the Holy Spirit.

Being inquisitive enough to experience new types of ministry without judgment.

- Growing in my understanding of truth and accurately assessing individual principles, ensuring my voice would not merely be dusty pontification, but would permeate the atmosphere with soundness, God's wisdom, and anointing.
- Learned sacrificial leadership from a particular mentor who spent his life shedding the behavioral skin of white privilege. This person trained me to be a Regional Minister and then affirmed my readiness, even when others fought against the idea.
- Living life intentionally and having fun *now*—a crucial reminder to embrace joy and not wait for a perfect time.

Family as Formation

Ultimately, my deepest formation came from my parents. My father, James Lee Melvin, the baby boy of four children, was a bishop and a pastor who was an enigma—always doing the unexpected and pushing ministry into new territories and onto new platforms. During his fifty-four years in ministry, he founded, co-founded, or built five churches, pastored three of them, and served as presiding bishop of the Goldsboro-Raleigh District Assembly, where growth and expansion were hallmarks. He was a prolific preacher and teacher, perpetually invested in the well-being of the community. Yet he loved his family fiercely: no matter where ministry took him, he was back home by Friday night to spend Saturday with his girls. He proudly bragged about his daughters' accomplishments to whoever would listen.

My mother, Ada Knight Melvin, was a force of nature: the youngest of nine children, intellectually gifted, and relationally generous. A proud alumna of Jarvis Christian College, she built a career that demonstrated relentless service. She dedicated thirty-one years to special education for the mentally disabled, served as chair of the board of directors for a women's recovery house, and held the visible role of First Lady of one of the largest African American congregations in our county. Crucially, despite these many responsibilities, she still lived out her own calling to domestic and foreign missions, eventually rising to become the national president of missions for the Church of Christ, Disciples of Christ, International. Her life was defined by the intersection of professional commitment, community advocacy, and global faith leadership.

Words like calling, anointing, study, preparation, and respect were not abstract ideas in our household; they were the rhythm of our daily life. My parents provided us with opportunities for exposure to life, culture, travel, recreation, languages, and ecumenical partnerships within and outside our city limits. I inherited this language of vocation from them. Yet, knowing the language of calling is one thing. Living into it—particularly as a Black woman in systems never designed with you in mind—is another.

Leadership and Titles

Leadership and titles in God's realm are two entirely different things. When people hear "Bishop Valerie Melvin," they do not know what to do with that title, especially when it rests on a Black woman who feels no compulsion to explain why she has answered God's call to this office. I have spent decades seeking, wrestling with my identity, and finally embracing who I truly am. I am not a bishop for prestige. I am a Bishop in the Lord's Church because it is one of the callings upon my life: to oversee, to serve, to teach, to build. I am a servant-leader, a listener, a bridge builder in places where others have erected walls. Serving as associate regional minister for eleven years and as regional minister for seven, I have come to understand deeply the slow, exhausting weight of cumulative disrespect—especially in predominantly White Christian spaces where many people remain unaware of their privilege. I serve a great number of Christian, well-meaning yet culturally unexamined White individuals who often believe they have the right to speak to me in a subordinate manner, their words laced with subtle disrespect, suspicion, or casual interrogation. They may not realize it, but their tone reveals the assumption that my leadership must constantly be proven, defended, or justified. Every conversation becomes an unspoken test: Can she answer quickly enough? Thoroughly enough? Confidently enough?

My legitimacy, it seems, must be demonstrated daily—through dialogue not of my own choosing, through debates I did not initiate, and through administrative excellence judged by standards not applied equally to others.

In these interactions, I am too often evaluated by everything *except* my calling, such as:

- the color of my skin
- my ability to explain or defend decisions that White leaders make without question
- my patience with disrespect disguised as inquiry
- my capacity to absorb critique without reciprocity
- my skills in administration, preaching, pastoral care, timeliness, and diplomacy—as if excellence in every single category is the only acceptable payment for my presence

And I do all of this without the support of an associate regional minister, a void that was not accidental. It was intentional—another version of the ancient expectation: make bricks without straw. It is the Pharaoh complex—demanding productivity without resourcing, demanding leadership without support, and demanding perfection without partnership. The system assumes I can carry the load alone, and then the system questions whether the weight I carry is evidence that I should be carrying it at all. This is the emotional and spiritual terrain I navigate daily. It is the unspoken wilderness of my calling. And yet, even in this wilderness, I lead. I listen. I serve. I build bridges across communities—many of whom have never had to consider how their privilege shapes their assumptions, expectations, and tone.

Although these experiences wound, they also clarify. They reveal the cultural and spiritual blindness that still haunts the Church. They remind me that part of my leadership is not only administrative or pastoral—it is prophetic. It is calling systems to account, naming truths that others prefer to leave unspoken, and refusing to shrink before the smallness of other people's expectations. And so, I carry on—not as Pharaoh's laborer, but as God's servant. Not as a subordinate to privilege, but as a steward of calling. Not as one questioned, but as one appointed.

Leadership has taken me into sacred and complicated spaces. My ministry spans three distinct but interconnected bodies: The Christian Church (Disciples of Christ), the Church of Christ, Disciples of Christ, International and the Piedmont District Convention. Each group carries its own history, identity, leadership, and expectations. The Region serves as the covenantal thread—an intricate role demanding diplomacy, cultural fluency, deep listening, and unwavering spiritual grounding.

My leadership story makes sense when I understand it as a tapestry woven by calling, community, and context. It is shaped by mentors—Black and White, Latinx and Asian, male and female—who saw possibility in me when I could not yet see it myself. Their wisdom remains in my decisions, values, and vision.

And through it all, I have survived storms—literal and figurative.

Here I Am—Still Standing

I made it through Hurricane Florence in 2018, when devastation swept across the Region.

I made it through the COVID-19 pandemic of 2020–2023, navigating grief, uncertainty, and a scattered Church.

I am still leading amid an unstable economy and unprecedented political fallout, where every decision carries new weight.

> Yet I am still here.
> Not by my own merit.
> Not because I am flawless or tireless.
> Not because I have mastered every challenge.
> I am here because the call is real.
> I am here because the God who called me has sustained me. The authority that sent me is the authority that keeps me.

Reflectively, my internal dialogue allowed me not just to endure such environments, but to lead within them. That dialogue rests on three core narratives.

First, I hold to a theology of inherent dignity. I believe that every person—including myself—is created by God with value and agency. In patriarchal structures, rigid family systems, or complex organizations where gendered expectations and long-standing power patterns can diminish or dismiss voices, that belief is my anchor. It reminds me that I do not enter any space begging for permission to exist or contribute. I enter as one whose presence, ideas, and leadership bear the imprint of divine intention.

Second, I commit to courageous presence. Leadership in resistant spaces is not just about speaking truth; it is about remaining whole while you do so. As disrespect is cumulative, exclusion can be subtle, coded, and systemic—like a slow-moving cloud trying to obscure who you truly are. In those moments, my internal voice says: *Show up anyway. Do not walk in the fear cast upon your ancestors, but in the bold expectation of their promise. Lead with the confidence of someone who belongs here.* That inner courage allows me to challenge injustice, advocate for equity, and model a leadership that is rooted in conviction rather than dominance.

Third, I practice disciplined self-reflection. Challenging environments can distort one's sense of self. They can tempt you to internalize negativity or adopt the very patterns you are called to transform. My internal questions—*What is mine to hold? What is mine to release? What is mine to transform?*—help me stay grounded. They keep me from living in perpetual reaction and remind me to align my actions with my purpose rather than with the dysfunction around me.

All these experiences are part of my soul story. Every person carries such a story—an unfolding narrative of memory, mystery, faith, challenge, and transformation. Constructing and celebrating that story is an act of spiritual courage. For me, constructing mine has meant pausing (with my therapist at my side) long enough to listen and learn from the moments that linger: the front porch with the dolls I called the Melvin Apostles, the voice on the football field, the classrooms filled with budding lives, the mentors who poured into me, the meetings where my voice was sidelined, and the altars where I surrendered. And finally, the place where I serve now with unending joy because I, Valerie Melvin am okay in my own skin!

In celebrating my story, I am not centering myself; I am stewarding the title and gifts for leadership that God placed in me and called out of me. My story is not just for me—it is a gift to others, a testimony that will help someone recognize the sacredness of their journey.

Wisdom for the Next Generation:

When I vacate this chair of Regional Minister and CEO of the Christian Church in North Carolina, I want to pass on the rod and the staff of pastoral ministry—symbols of strength, protection, and guidance—to those coming after me.

The Rod (Support and Strength): Teaching women when to lean on the rod for support emphasizes self-care and community reliance. It teaches them that their authority does not demand tireless, self-sacrificing perfection (the Pharaoh complex). They must find strength in their internal dialogue and the companions they choose.

The Staff (Guidance and Direction): Teaching with the staff for guidance means leading with soundness, God's wisdom, and anointing. This is the prophetic function—directing the people toward righteousness and truth. It requires patience not passivity, but wisdom and the ability to be radical yet rooted, ensuring that change is purposeful, not simply reactive.

My heart desires for women in ministry to exercise such strong discernment that they can smell the stench of the "old guard," which raises its head every time the Church undergoes transformation. This guard grabs power by imposing rules that they themselves are not willing to follow—rules never made for them, but for the rest of us. I want women emerging in ministry to push back at this enemy of the Church's unity by forging ahead, preaching prophetically, teaching strategically, and using spiritual and intellectual skills to set the generation coming behind you free. Like the great abolitionist, Harriet Tubman, who led 13 Underground Railroad excursions to liberate enslaved people, let us:

- be radical, yes—but also rooted.
- speak truth—but with timing.
- take risks—and to honor rest.

Sharing this wisdom ensures that the next generation does not need to repeat the mistakes of those who came before them. Rather, they can use their divinely appointed roles to be bridge builders for all God's people.

A Final Word

Step carefully, ladies, there's glass everywhere! Ministry often extracts high prices. It is both beautiful and hard, and thus we are not meant to do this work alone. Choose wisely. Sharing the ministry alongside someone who loves you deeply, who can laugh with you and lift you, makes the journey sweeter. I have walked many years single, and I have made peace with that. But if love finds you, let it hold you.

This amazing journey with sisters of color in leadership has reminded me that I am not alone. I have learned to laugh at and then reclaim the introverted and deeply felt parts of myself. I feel, love, and lead deeply. And by the grace of God, I am still learning, growing, being shaped deeply. At sixty-five, with thirty years of ministry behind me, I have lost interest in perfection. I am pursuing purpose. God has called me, formed me, and led me to being a bridge builder—and that is not a metaphor for me; it is the core of my ministry. I build bridges between generations, across race and gender lines, and between theological divides. I invite people into covenantal conversation, into those "come, let us reason together" moments where truth and grace meet.

When it is all said and done—if my life has encouraged one soul, reconciled one rift, or built one bridge that helped someone cross into their calling empowered by God's divine design of their authenticity—then I will be ready to come in from my front porch, put the dolls away and rest.

— ***Bishop Valerie Melvin*** *is the Regional Minister and CEO of the Christian Church (Disciples of Christ) in North Carolina.*

Where I Am From

Formed, Nurtured, and Shaped by Community

Rev. Teresa "Terri" Hord Owens

Steeped in Family and Faith

To understand my story, you must have some knowledge of where I am from. I am a descendant of two of the oldest free Black settlements in Indiana: my maternal line in Lost Creek, just outside Terre Haute, and my paternal line in Westfield, just north of Indianapolis. Both settlements were established in the early 19th century, around the 1820s and 1830s. I grew up with both sets of grandparents; my maternal grandparents were still very much a part of the historic Lost Creek community. My maternal grandmother poured the history of the community into me at every turn. I was surrounded by people who were aunts, uncles, and cousins—relatives beyond my immediate family who taught me that no matter how far away we might be on the family tree, we were kin.

Terre Haute was a town of about 80,000 people when I was born, about 7% Black. Despite the presence of strong state universities like Indiana State (Terre Haute), Indiana University (Bloomington), and Purdue (Lafayette), along with prestigious private colleges like Wabash, (Crawfordsville), Earlham (Richmond), and St. Mary-of-the Woods (Terre Haute), Indiana was the heart of the resurgence of the Ku Klux Klan in the 1920s, and stories of their terror were known to me. Racial tensions manifested at football and basketball games against schools in other parts of Indiana. We understood there were certain communities that were not safe for Black people.

My sense of myself was shaped in my home, my family, and my church. My paternal grandfather, a local Baptist pastor, had been involved in the efforts to desegregate public restaurants and social spaces. Our church had a strong ministry to the three colleges in the area, and my grandfather was known for his relevant, community- and justice-oriented ministry. My father taught junior high, then high school, where he coached national debate champions. By the time I was about 10, we were required to read one book per week by or about Black people. In the context of a community that was 93% white, I was raised in a household where my Black identity was being affirmed, educated, and encouraged. I was raised in a church where the pastor, my grandfather, had worked for the desegregation of public facilities, led the effort to build a community center in the Black community, and was continuously engaged in ecumenical and interfaith dialogue. I began my life's journey having my identify affirmed and in the care of those who believed it was their job to equip me to be whole as a little Black girl and subsequently a Black woman in America.

I was steeped in the Christian faith. Both sets of grandparents attended and were active in church. I went to Sunday School every week, followed by morning worship, whatever afternoon program might be happening, and then Baptist Training Union, every Sunday at 6:00 pm. I went to Vacation Bible School. I participated in youth activities in my congregation and the conference to which we belonged in the Baptist church. I was a delegate to the Indiana Sunday School and BTU Congress the summer I was 12. I was in all the plays and drama pieces that my paternal grandmother organized and produced. I watched proudly as the church warmly embraced college students, largely due to my grandfather's relevant ministry and care for young people. I was given leadership opportunities early in church, whether it was playing the piano for Sunday School devotion, Vacation Bible School, or serving on the Junior Usher Board, joining other youth to visit nursing homes and supporting those who had food insecurity. I grew up in a church where justice meant love in action, where the pastor was not afraid to tell the truth or confront the white community truthfully. Children and youth were respected and honored. Every week in the bulletin, a prayer written by a child was featured. Each year on Youth Day, a young person was invited to be the speaker. One year, I was a Youth Day speaker, and I was allowed to stand in the pulpit. At the time, there were no female ministers in my context, so I didn't realize how significant that was. There were various guest female speakers for special days, but not pastors. Years later when I acknowledged my call to ministry, I reflected on the fact that my grandfather had never prevented a woman from standing in the pulpit. He met my own call with warmth, love, and support, contrary to the ways in which many Black male Baptist pastors later responded to me and the ways in which many of our current ecumenical partners around the world do not recognize women in ordained ministry.

Moments of Truth

My dad always taught us that we must speak up for ourselves and others, but we needed to be equipped to do so. If you had a different opinion than the teacher, you needed to cite your own reading and research that had led to your conclusions. My first public stand for justice happened in the fifth grade. I was selected for the gifted student program. Another Black girl and I were the first and only Black students in the cohort of about 25 in fifth grade. Having come from a neighborhood school, I was used to having more Blacks in class, but I adapted to being one of two. American History is a central part of the curriculum in fifth grade, and our pedagogical model was very Montessori-like: we had many projects where we were given the freedom to pursue our studies at our own pace, according to our own interests. We still gathered to listen to the teacher read and we had class meetings. On this occasion, we were discussing the content for a play about American history. We had decided to have a time machine. In the midst of our conversation, one girl shouted out, "That's a horrible thing to say!" The teacher, Mrs. Black (yes, that was her name!), responded, "Why don't you share that conversation with the whole class?"

The girl replied, "John said we should have Terri and Susan playing slaves picking cotton in the play."

I could feel the blood rushing to my head, and I immediately stood up and said, "John, if you want slaves picking cotton, you better pick it your d*** self!" The rest of the class was stunned, then they started laughing because I used a curse word. I didn't normally use curse words, and of course my parents were summoned later for a conference with the teacher. My mother was all about self-control and discipline, but my dad told the teacher, "She has not been raised to allow her Blackness to be made fun of. She is one of two Black students in the class, and you cannot expect that she would say nothing in response." Mrs. Black asked my dad to work with our class on how we could include Black history in our time machine. I recited Langston Hughes' poem, "The Negro Mother," as a way of embodying the experience from a Black perspective. My parents had stood with me, and my dad turned an ugly moment into an opportunity for others to learn and for me and my Black classmate to be clothed in the dignity of history spoken in truth. My outburst was honored, too—my parents never punished me. The incident became a part of my learning about what it means to be Black in the United States.

In sixth grade, there was another moment of truth. Our program had been moved to a different school, and the playground had a huge tree stump where we liked to gather during recess. The rule we had for ourselves was whoever reached the stump first—the girls or the boys—would own the stump for that recess. One day, the girls won. One of the boys came up to us and said, "Time for you all to let us have the stump."

My response was, "We have rules and we must abide by them. This is a country of laws, and we have freedoms."

The little boy walked over to me, got in my face, and said, "What do you know about freedom? If it weren't for us White people, you n*****s would still be slaves."

I snapped back, "What did you just call me?" I was angry!

He got even closer to my face, and said, "I said, 'n*****'!" He then slapped me in the face, hard enough to knock off my wireframed eyeglasses, causing the lenses to shatter across my face and cheeks. The girls were horrified, and soon everyone was shouting.

I ran into the school office and defiantly told the school secretary, "Call my mom!"

"What happened?" she asked. "Joe called me a n*****! Call my mom!"

My mom came, and I went home. This was before the days of LensCrafters, so it took nearly two weeks for me to get new glasses. The classmate knocked on my door one day and stood there with his dad. He had come to apologize, and his father paid for my new glasses. This student and I went to the same junior and senior high schools and were ultimately among the group of eight valedictorians in our high school graduating class. But we never really engaged in any kind of conversation, and to me he remained the enemy.

Whenever I tell these stories, I feel the trauma response in my body all over again. I have used these stories as part of storytelling events, sermon illustrations, and sharing in icebreakers. I shared this story in response to the prompt, "Share a time when you started to understand who you were." I can now name the trauma, both physical and emotional, particularly of the 6th-grade experience when I was struck, hit hard in the face, and had my glasses shattered on my face. This is racial violence, both to the body and the soul. That 12-year-old little Black girl is inside me. I have tried to make sure that she can be sophisticated and wise in her responses to the trauma that arises in womanhood, but she is still there. That little girl stood up for dignity and told the truth, and she was attacked physically and called the n-word. My fellow Black student is still a good friend to this day. She has told me on many occasions that she was always amazed by my courage to speak up in those moments. She grew up in a family where her father wanted to shield her. Their family lived in an all-white neighborhood. I was one of her only Black friends. Unlike me, she had not been equipped to face the inevitable attacks on our dignity and humanity. That 12-year-old little girl still stands to say, "That's not right!" and "What did you just say?" My passion for justice has come from these places and these experiences. Only in recent years have I come to understand how profoundly that physical and emotional trauma has helped shape who I am today. That 12-year-old Terri is inside me.

The Faithfulness of God

I never imagined I would become a minister. I had been very active in the Junior Achievement program, so my first thought for college was to study business administration or economics. I changed my major from economics to government/political science in my sophomore year, and it made a huge difference in how I engaged in my studies. I was an active lay leader at my church during the summer, and the summer after my sophomore year, my family joined a Disciples congregation in Indianapolis. Although my grandfather had long been a leader in the Indiana State Sunday School and Baptist Training Union Congress, he did not exercise any overt influence on this decision. Some friends who had belonged to our church in Terre Haute had joined what was then Second Christian Church and invited us to visit. We found the pastor, Dr. Tom Benjamin Jr., had a similar prophetic focus as my grandfather. Later known as Light of the World Christian Church, this church offered Bible study every single day of the week. You could not be an elder, deacon, teacher or any kind of leader unless you were in a regular Bible study. This is not to say the study was dogmatic. It was very "Disciple" in that everyone was encouraged to be equipped to understand the text and to be able to discern the Biblical truths for themselves with the help of the Holy Spirit. That commitment to Biblical literacy remains one of focal points in Light of the World's ministry. The church was also involved in the Black community and hosted many community events. The community-mindedness of the pastor and congregation drew many Black leaders to be a part of the congregation.

Up to this point in my life, I was the wife of someone in ministry and was considered an asset to his ministry. I was totally fine with that. I was increasingly disillusioned with my corporate world, but I felt if my career and salary could afford Walter the opportunity to do what he truly loved, then I was glad to be able to support him. However, I increasingly grew resentful that he was able to live out his calling, and I was stuck in a career that, while offering significant financial benefits, did nothing to provide me with a sense of fulfillment. I even felt guilty for having these feelings. Anyone who knows Walter knows he was and has been doing exactly what he was created to do. He was not the one standing in the way of my fulfillment—I was.

On March 31, 1996, Palm Sunday, I led the children's choir in a dramatic musical presentation of Jesus' Triumphal Entry into Jerusalem. Dr. Benjamin had been doing a sermon series, exhorting people to acknowledge and accept their calls to ministry. Mind you, I had avoided church on several Sundays while he was doing this series. Walter, my Eli, kept saying, "Terri, God is speaking to you." I could not accept this. Every time I was in church during that series, I was uncomfortable and couldn't enjoy the worship. On this particular Sunday, when the invitation to discipleship was being given, I felt a presence that literally lifted me by the collar of my dress and pushed me forward down the aisle. I had never had such a sense of something beyond myself. Others said it looked like I was stumbling forward, and I didn't look physically stable.

I lurched up to the pastor, who asked, "Are you ok?"

I said, "I need to accept my call to ministry."

He smiled and offered me a big hug. As we stood there while the invitation continued, my mother came up to stand next to me. She put her arm around me and asked, "Are you ok?"

"Yes," I replied. "I have to accept my call to ministry."

"It's about time," she said, and gave me a huge hug. My husband joined us at the altar and began to lift his hands in praise. Once the pastor described what had happened, the congregation applauded. That day and the memory of the Spirit lifting me and moving me down the aisle will remain with me always.

I saw God's faithfulness in new ways in those years as I journeyed to Chicago to attend the University of Chicago Divinity School. My fears that my schooling would take time away from my son never materialized. He was in the third grade when I started and was old enough to understand homework. I studied when he did. I read and wrote papers while waiting for him during his percussion ensemble lessons and rehearsals and while waiting to pick him from Chicago Children's Choir rehearsals. In the summer, when he played soccer, I was free from classes and able to be that ultimate soccer mom. He learned the Greek alphabet with me that first week of classes and took it to school for show and tell. He bragged to his fourth grade teacher that his mom was reading books that were 1,000 pages long. This was true—I had one course where the smallest book was 500 pages. Now 35, a husband and father of an almost 3-year-old boy, he remembers only that his mom was in graduate school when he was in elementary school, and his testimony is that, "She always made sure I was good, that I was ok. She was there."

I know so many women in ministry today are second-career and may be juggling family and work responsibilities along with necessary seminary studies. I am blessed to have a life partner who has stood firmly and walked enthusiastically with me every step of the way. I share this story because the fear that my family would suffer caused me to delay answering my call. All I can say is that if it is God who is calling, God will provide, make ways, and give you strength, and when you look back, you will have to shout because you will know it was God who kept you.

Wisdom for the Next Generation

A big part of my story is learning to be comfortable with my own voice in preaching as a Black woman who grew up under her grandfather's pastorate. My grandfather was more of a classical preacher. He didn't whoop. He was always entertaining and interesting, well-prepared, poetic, and erudite. I was never a whooper either, and my style of preaching has never and will never be like some of the great Black women preachers in our society, whom I greatly admire for their preaching gifts. For many years, that understanding of myself kept me from thinking that I was called to preach. I never thought I would be received preaching in a Black context. I wanted to teach in congregations and possibly at the seminary level. But once I started preaching at the church my husband served, I learned people remembered my sermons and enjoyed them. "I remember what you say," many would share with me. "Sometimes a preacher says a whole lot, but I don't remember what they said." I have learned that God can use me, just as I am, in the way and manner that I preach, to deliver God's truth, inspiration, encouragement, challenge, and hope. Rev. Dr. Gardner Taylor, often called the Dean of Black preaching said that, "Preaching is truth through personality." He always emphasized the importance of authenticity and using one's unique voice and personality to preach the gospel. It is most important to bring yourself to the task of preaching, but as Dr. Gardner would always say, you have to recognize that you are a flawed vessel bringing the message of the gospel. The message must be relevant to the context of those you are preaching. This understanding has helped me become comfortable with my preaching voice, and comfortable with myself and my understanding of what my own ministry is.

Black women are familiar with the stereotype of the angry Black woman. Women in general are often called bossy and aggressive when they voice opinions strongly or when they lean into their own agency in leadership. Women who are comfortable with authority are often misunderstood in an environment where accountability and authority are held suspect. I have a lot of experience as a Black woman leading in predominantly White corporate and higher education environments. I am used to being the "first" or the "only one." The realities of racism in our society have not left the church untouched. I have watched many of my sisters of color be underestimated, disrespected, and put in a corner. The assumption often is that because we have not seen your kind in this place before, you must not be prepared to be in this place. My answer is that I have been in many places that have prepared me for leadership, far more than many of my current colleagues. When you are clear about your gifts, skills, experience, and what you bring to the table, never apologize for being all that you are. Never apologize for being qualified, talented, and capable. It is not your job to make them comfortable with the wonder that God has wrought in you.

Knowing who you are is crucial. Your understanding of your own identity must be so intrinsic to your way of being that you will not allow others to misunderstand, ignore or disrespect the very real heritage and background that you bring to a role in ministry or anywhere in leadership. Read all you can, not only about theology and philosophy, but about the history of your people. Stand ready to speak the truth about that history, and be clear what it means to identify as Black.

Just as we need to know who we are, we need to be firm in *whose* we are. It will not be enough that you are a powerful speaker. You must be grounded in a relationship with the Divine that equips and strengthens you for the work. Spiritual practice is essential; you need prayer time, mediation—time with the Holy One. Knowledge of Scripture is also essential. You cannot preach the Word of God unless you not only love it but know it and respect it, too. You must allow it to seep into your very bones, feeding you with wisdom that will develop as a result of your commitment to it. There will be times when our own human insecurities and frailties threaten to derail us and get the better of us. If we are not rooted and grounded in spiritual practice and the Word, we will be all the more vulnerable to situations that come to threaten and destroy not only our witness but our very personhood.

We do not do ministry or life alone. Whether you have a partner or not, you must have friends who are there for you, who understand you, who will pray for you, who will be a safe space for you to shout, cry, vent, rejoice, and celebrate. In this world, it matters that you have a village of people who are like you, not just those who like you. It still matters to have a community of those who share your culture, your race, your identity, even as you seek to stay at the table with those whose views and background are divergent from your own. Take time to develop friendships and strong collegial relationships. Know whether you can trust a person before divulging all you know or allowing yourself to be vulnerable. Everyone who looks like you is not for you. Ask God for a discerning spirit as to whom you can entrust your confidence and with whom you share friendship. If your life is one of spiritual practice and you are biblically grounded, you need someone of like mind to share space with and to walk the journey with you. Finding "your people" is often a hard task but do the work to build the relationships.

A Final Word

The Scripture that has grounded me for more than two decades now is Philippians 1:6, "I am confident of this, that the one who began a good work in you will continue to complete it until the day of Jesus Christ" (NRSV). There are wonderful people in the world, in the church, and certainly in my life. But my confidence is not placed in them, despite my great love and respect for so many. Ultimately, I must stand on my understanding of God's will and God's way, even when others doubt me. Even when others disagree, we must have confidence in the God who made us and know that God will equip us with the wisdom and strength to stay at the table, to work for a more equitable world and church for all. It is from that confidence that I proceed, not under my own steam. The ancestors would say, "Know that you know that you know." Be who you say you are, daughter and woman of God. Know who you are and *whose* you are and never apologize. You are fearfully and wonderfully made, as Psalm139 tells you. Perhaps not like others in looks, sound, or gifting. But you are the Lord's. I have learned to stand in that confidence in God, and I pray for God's strength to continue to be all that God has created me to be.

— ***Rev. Terri Hord Owens*** *is the first African American woman to lead the Christian Church (Disciples of Christ) in the United States and Canada. At the time of her election in 2017, she was the first African American woman to lead a mainline denomination and serve as head of communion.*

Many Rivers to Cross

A Black Woman's Summation About Her Leadership, Spirituality, and Community

Rev. Dr. Christal L. Williams

The Strength and Beauty of Black Women

I am deeply grateful for the opportunity to contribute to the expanding spaces of love, learning, and leadership created to center and empower Black women. It is about time we receive our due—our flowers, support, pedestals, and checks. Black women are the most underrated and underestimated group in the system. It is time to give proper recognition and regard to Black women for who they are and for how they have built, birthed, and brokered for all human demographics.

They manage to do it with deep spirituality, innate passion, and a strong commitment to developing personal and professional agency to navigate the present and future. She has a secret: With the help of God and her ancestors, she will overcome any obstacles thrown her way.

For my own sake, you will find nestled within these pages my own moments of transparency and an open testimony of my journey toward leadership. What is written here comes from my passion, steeped with a mixture of generational perseverance and the power of prayer. The words you read are in my voice because it proves to me that pain, pleasure, courage, and contention can co-exist and help another woman along the way.

I love Black women. I come from the many shapes, ideas, and colors that help to make up my family of origin. I think of one of my grandmothers, who had sandy red hair, and my great-grandmother, who carried African and Indian features and traits. To me, this is a gift from God. We get to see genetic ingenuity at work, up close and personal. The many cultures from which we are molded and shaped are amazing. I placed the '*s*' on cultures because we have our families of origin, communities of choice, geographic locations, social norms, and much more that defines us. I am aware that while people, places, and situations often attempt to represent us, they usually do so inaccurately. For the sake of accountability and responsibility, I ask: Who truly gets to define me—me and every waking, life-altering experience I encounter? No one gets to tell the story of my life or current personal or professional whereabouts other than me.

The story of my life and ministry can't be fully told in a few pages. But what I will share is God's faithfulness and strengthening love of community. From the moment I responded to God's call in 1974 to my current role in ministry fifty-one years later, I've been committed to following the plan set for me. This chapter wouldn't be worth reading if I didn't admit—there have been rejections, failures, and times when I felt like I was sinking.

I resonate with André Crouch's song, *Through It All*, "I've had many tears and sorrows, and questions for my tomorrow...through it all I have learned to trust..." Trusting God and the process guides me daily in my work as a Regional Minister. It is the tenacity deep within my soul that allows my vision for my work to move forward. It is not easy, but it is worth it.

In June 2011, pop and rhythm and blues singer Ledisi released the album "Pieces of Me." It features the hit song *Bravo,* a shoutout of affirmation and approval for women. The song calls women to a place of honesty about who they were and the big moves they were planning to make in life and love. I appreciate the song because it serves as an anthological sourcebook, carrying a clarion call for all women to stand up and claim all opportunities to celebrate who they are and what they bring to all tables where they sit.

Yes, I have been loved, honored, and not without the sacred scars on my heart and body serving as evidence of my struggles and triumphs. They earned me the right to stand and be called a leader. Leadership is in our very bones as Black women. We innately carry in our wombs the ideas, expressions, and principles of leadership. At other times, the leader within us is inherited from our ancestors. Dr. Yolanda Pierce, in her book, *In My Grandmother's House: Black Women, Faith and the Stories We Inherit,* speaks to the powerful insight of women who never received a formal education but can be counted upon as Black Women theologians. Those women who have surrounded us in love, wisdom, sacrifice, and sacramental exchange. Women who have given of their own heart, money, spirituality, and faith in helping us to steer better what we could not do for ourselves. This starts very early in life.

My only proof of my inherited leadership is from what I have seen and experienced on the playground. From serving as leaders to our siblings to being line leaders in elementary school, during recess, someone always emerges as a leader. The spirit of leadership is captured early in our childhood. It is developed and strengthened with every step we take. From learning to clean the kitchen and put dinner on the stove to running a district, region, or even a denomination, leadership is always germinating in and around us.

In this segment of my life, as preacher, prophet, and president, I must be honest and tell you that there have been many nights when I have sung Mahalia Jackson's version of the spiritual, "How I Got Over." The people God has sent into my life have helped usher me to places seen and unseen. Their collection of hands that have helped and continue to help me navigate the terrain of life and ministry. (Thanks be to God.) Hands are used for shaping, structuring, and holding that clay on the wheel until it is just right. The potter's wheel, although full of movement, is in some ways a place of critical stability.

Black women everywhere continue to be shaped by the power of their work, love, the struggle, their resilience, and liberation. From the days of Assata Shakur, Audre Lorde, and Shirley Chisholm, the voices of women leave trails of breadcrumbs for the next generation to follow. This is capacity building at its best. No one arrives by themselves. In life, there is a humming of growth, and that, ever so softly yet persistently, leads and has led me into places known and to be known. If you ever want to know where leadership is located, it is situated in areas where people's shoulders are squared, their vision is unobstructed, and their courage is unwavering. Leadership is the place where bravery stands against the winds of inequity and injustice and demanding payment.

I realize being a leader is not without a cost. An old Jimmy Cliff song, "Many Rivers to Cross," song describes someone who is traveling and cannot seem to find their way. But the traveler is determined to keep their pride. In many ways, the song effectively depicts some of the experiences of Black women. It lays out the way we love, lead, and make decisions, which often costs us our own dignity, integrity, and pride. Oleta Adams sang a remake of this song in the 1994 movie "Jason's Lyric." I like the elevated rendition of the song. The lyrics and the meaning were the same, but the tempo changed. This new version was sung by a woman who offered not just feelings of being stuck and without a way home. It was sung with possibilities and probabilities in mind. It spoke to me personally, not as a voice of mystery and fear, but as a connection and with resolve. In life and leadership, one must develop a resolve to move through adversity, understanding that there is a way out, a way through, and a way back. Black women have crossed many rivers—muddy, mighty, swollen rivers. We have done so armed only with faith, purpose, and the strength of our past, determined to reach our futures.

For me, leadership has never been about my arrival but about the journey I share with others. As I have travelled, I've listened, created, built, loved, and led. One could call it emergence; out of emergence comes the word "emergency." What is an emergency? An urgent need for assistance or relief. After thirty years of professional ministry, I am still emerging—and sometimes, it is an emergency. An urgent need to allow that which is holy, sacred, and loving to be released into my space or the place where others reside. There are times when I, with hands outstretched, need to produce for others, even when I am not at my best, but I cross the river to serve as God has called me to do.

The Rivers We've Crossed

Growing up in Cleveland, Ohio, I was most familiar with two significant bodies of water: Lake Erie, one of the Great Lakes, and the Cuyahoga River. The Cuyahoga River flows in a U-shape throughout the northeastern region of Ohio before emptying into Lake Erie. Most people are familiar with the Cuyahoga River due to its infamous 1969 fire. The damage was caused by all the pollutants, chemicals, and trash the steel mills emptied into it. Today, it is slowly being restored, and people are enjoying the cleaned-up waterway that was once the eyesore of a state.

The first river I crossed was at the age of four, when baptized at Gray's Temple Baptist Church. It was my family's church, founded by my ancestors, who were part of the Great Migration from Alabama. Not only did they bring their children, hopes, and dreams North, they brought their deep spirituality, passionate faith, and precious hope for the future.

The church was organized and dedicated in my maternal great-grandmother's living room. She was indeed the matriarch of the church, and her family was there to fill in the gaps. One could say that I naturally slide into my role as a pastor, and such spirituality was already part of my DNA. By age six, I was discussing my call story with my grandfather, the chairman of the Deacon Board, who insisted that God must call me three times.

I remember clearly the night I marched into my grandparents' bedroom and informed them that God had called me three times, and I could articulate each time. They told me God did not call women. From that moment, I heard in my heart the sound of doors closing and glass ceilings being shattered. My grandfather's understanding of scripture did not stop me. Neither did my call distract him. After sharing with him my desire to preach, he made sure I had a leadership role in everything our church did, from giving Easter speeches to serving as Junior Church Secretary.

In the late 1980s and early 1990s, my grandfather developed Alzheimer's disease. It led to his total incapacitation, and he could only communicate by blinking his eyes. One evening, I returned home from college to visit him. We had a gentle moment. The woman I was then and the six-year girl that had announced her call whispered in his ear, "You know I am called to preach." I do not know why I did that, but the family patriarch and my father-figure blinked. Maybe because, for once in my life, he couldn't verbally stop this call or maybe he was telling me he and God were going to talk about his granddaughter either way, it is a moment I cherish. In 1992, he died.

After the funeral, everyone returned to my grandmother's home for a meal. I walked around serving drinks until two of my elderly aunts invited me to join their conversation. I wondered what type of shenanigans they were up to as they insisted that I sit with them. After I sat down, they never spoke directly to me. Yet I listened intently to a conversation that apparently had been going on for several minutes before my arrival. They were speaking in coded language, and I couldn't understand the topic or the plot of the story. However, I stuck around long enough to realize they were talking about my life and where they saw me heading. I later learned they were speaking prophetically about my future. These two mystics were conspiring with God and the universe about my future! At one point during the conversation, Aunt Hattie from Ashtabula said, "I see you going across many rivers."

Not knowing what to think, how to feel, or ways to respond, I sat in silence. The thoughts running through my brain were so loud, I could almost hear them outside of my head. Was Aunt Hattie confident it was me? I had only ever known the Cuyahoga River and Lake Erie. Who knew that the magic of her words would send my life on an unexpected trajectory?

The metaphor of many rivers to cross is deeply real for me. Aunt Hattie's words pointed not only to literal rivers I would cross but also to the invisible, restless rivers of racism, patriarchy, exclusion, poverty, and silence. Did Aunt Hattie realize I couldn't swim? How would I rise to embrace the blessings of her words? How would I plug the hole in the bottom of my boat? I would go on to face the waters of White supremacy, fragility, favoritism, and systemic oppression.

I began crossing those rivers at a young age. I was the first to do many things: the first African American girl to integrate the Girl Scout troop outside of Philadelphia, the first and only African American to serve as a children's ministry intern at a predominantly White congregation in Indiana, the first African American woman to serve as regional minister and president of the Christian Church in Tennessee. With every first, there have been blessings and turbulence—creating tides so high that crossing those rivers seemed impossible at first glance.

The uneven road toward leadership was rarely paved. But God! The road to leadership is often walked barefoot on stones of doubt, under the scorching gaze of scrutiny. Yet the love of God and the sunshine of community have always carried me safely to the other side. As a child, I loved reading about Harriet Tubman and others who paved the way for success. From Sojourner Truth declaring, "Ain't I a woman?" to Fannie Lou Hamer's righteous indignation to my own unapologetic trailblazing, Black women have always made a way out of no way because it was necessary. "Making a way out of no way" was a motto in my single-parent home. My mother had a way of making something out of nothing. Whether it was providing food on the table, clothes on our backs, or toys under the Christmas tree, my mother was the queen of making ways out of no way. Her strong faith and her resolve were built upon the shoulders of the mothers who came before her. Those women understood the importance of taking care of business—taking care of the home, the children, and the rent. This was my first glimpse of leadership.

In the poem *The Negro Speaks of Rivers,* Langston Hughes wrote, "I've known rivers ancient as the world and older than the flow of human blood in human veins. My soul has grown deep like the rivers." I, too, have known those rivers. They have run through my experiences with church structures and politics. I have navigated the cold waters of male-dominated boardrooms and classrooms. I have swum before the shallow waters of race prejudice, plus the misuse of power found in systems and institutions. I have seen the frailty of elections. The rivers have been a constant presence throughout my entire life, and they run through my own spirit, calling me repeatedly to leadership with unwavering faith and a resilient mindset.

When God called me to ministry, I did not leap into the waters with the confidence I had as a child. At age twenty-three, when I realized I would enter seminary in preparation for ministry, I wrestled. I questioned. I pushed back against the current. But the call persisted—sometimes as a whisper in the quiet of my spirit, other times as a roar I could not ignore. Eventually, I surrendered—not out of defeat, but out of sacred and holy trust in knowing whom God calls, God equips; realizing that God, who begins a good work in us, is faithful to complete the action.

Deep Spirituality: The Source Beneath the Surface

In the Book of Revelation, it is written: "Then the angel showed me the river of the water of life, as clear as crystal, flowing from the throne of God and of the Lamb" (Revelation 22:1, NIV). If Black women are placed in rivers that are expected to flow, then we must remember that our spirituality is the sacred trust that finds the underground springs from which we originate.

For generations, Black women have drawn deeply from the well of spiritual truth—a theology that holds both the lament of the wilderness and the liberation of the promised land. Our spirituality is not performance; it is provision and preservation. It is the prayers of our mothers, the songs of our ancestors, and the sermons we preach with our lives. Deep spirituality is how we breathe, how we resist, how we reclaim our dignity. It encourages us to trust God for what we need to get by. I grew up with the song "Got Any Rivers?" Oscar C. Eliason wrote, "Have you any rivers that seem uncrossable? And do you have any mountains through which you cannot plow? God specializes in things thought impossible. And He will do what no other power—holy ghost power can do."

This is the same song my grandfather sang in a rich baritone voice. He would lean over and say, "God specializes." Although he was steeped within the traditions of the day, even he understood that Jesus could do what no other power could do! (Can I get a witness?) I express with great certainty that God truly does specialize. God has equipped and is equipping while supplying what's needed for the journey. God is closing the gap that tries to prevent us from moving forward. For years, I was bound up, silenced by my own fears and shortcomings. But my freedom finally arrived, and that was when I knew that my faithfulness paid off.

How did all of this happen? It happened that day I gave God my yes. It happened when I was knee deep in the scratchy waters of life. My surrender, my yes, would encourage my persistence as I waded through the waters of leadership.

Creating Space: Sacred Hospitality

Dr. Howard Thurman, a pastor, mystic, and theologian, writes about the practice of hospitality. I recognize Thurman in the mystic practices gifted to me by my mother Norma Jean, my aunt Hattie Carlton and my grandmother, Lula Mae. Well before I read his book *The Search for Common Ground,* I was being raised by these women to encounter the sacred. Like these women, Thurman invited me to consider what it meant to create sacred encounters where the host and the guest are transformed. He explains that hospitality provides a mutual exchange that forms the basis for experiencing deep empathy and connection. He describes it as "the sound of the genuine, allowing true pilgrimage into the other person's heart."

Each time Jesus was with the Disciples, there was an intimacy and a confidential space for sharing, learning, eating, and making miracles. As I read scripture, the hospitality offered during those encounters can be compared to the hush harbors that those enslaved created to survive the conditions they faced. Hush harbors are necessary. They were made to do the business of the ministry of healing and deliverance needed to live another day. There were hush harbors created for my survival. There were hush harbors created for my deliverance and my liberation. That's why the sacredness of love and hospitality is a recipe for success.

The entry of friendship, confidentiality, prayer, and openness covers and fortifies Black women. The community provides the necessary space for sharing among those who genuinely have the same interests at heart. It is a matter of safety, solidarity, and care for the recipients. In a society that centers Whiteness and maleness as the default, creating space is a radical and holy act. It allows Black women to be fully themselves—not mimicking cultural expectations and expressions that are not wholly their own. Creating spaces allows Black women to do things differently while standing in divine authenticity. We create space at the kitchen table, in church pews, in boardrooms, and behind pulpits. Sometimes, we create space wherever our souls lead us. Creating space is not only about programs and policies; it is also about posture. It is listening more than speaking, centering those pushed to the margins, declaring with our presence: You belong.

Black Women Leading: Because of Who We Are

Too often, Black women's leadership is framed as "despite." However, the truth is that we lead because of who we are. We lead because of the communities we love and the faith we embody. Leadership is often born out of the struggles we know and the adversity we've faced. We lead movements, not just meetings. We cast visions, not just votes. We organize, strategize, and mobilize. And we do so collectively, raising one another, mentoring, midwifing, and mothering each other's callings.

Our leadership is not accidental—it is anointed. To write off Black women in leadership is to name the tension between joy and exhaustion, calling and constraint. And yet, we hold hope. Not naïve optimism, but resurrection hope. A hope that says even if the world does not make space, we will build it ourselves—with bricks of love and mortar of resistance. We believe in a God who parts waters, yes—but also in a God who gives us strength to swim. Here's that river again. It appears once more in this story, inviting me to cross it.

Wisdom For the Next Generations

My leadership has fostered many partnerships, collaborations, friendships, and mentorships. I will be the first to acknowledge that my life and career were made easier at the hands of many—those important cheerleaders who helped lead me down the waterway. Remembering these important leaders is part of the sacredness of the entire experience. Cole Arthur Riley writes, "I don't want to make it to the promised land if it means I forget the wilderness." He adds, "When you practice remembrance, you're traveling into stories and reminding yourself what it looks like to go on." I believe part of my role is to share some of the strategies I've been given. They are an invitation to join me and others as we continue to grow together as we cross many rivers.

Ten Steps for a Successful Black Woman

1. Self-Awareness: Knowing Who You Are
Leadership begins with identity—knowing you are fearfully and wonderfully made, created in God's image, and called with purpose. Through prayer and reflection, leaders discern their strengths and areas of growth. "Search me, O God, and know my heart; test me and know my thoughts." (Psalm 139:23, NRSV)

2. Vision: Seeing Oneself with God's Eyes
A leader seeks God's and the community's guidance to help shape a vision that uplifts the team while aligning with divine purpose. Vision is not self-serving; it is serving the organization wherein one serves. "Where there is no prophecy, the people cast off restraint, but happy are those who keep the law." (Proverbs 29:18, NRSV)

3. Communication: Speak Truth in Love
Words have the power to build up or tear down. Spirit-led leaders communicate with grace, honesty, and compassion, always seeking to reflect God's love. "Let your speech always be gracious, seasoned with salt, so that you may know how you ought to answer everyone." (Colossians 4:6, NRSV)

4. Action: Walk in Faith and Integrity

Leadership requires bravery. It needs courage and consistency—doing justice, showing mercy, and living with integrity. Actions speak louder than titles. "He has told you, O mortal, what is good; and what does the Lord require of you but to do justice, and to love kindness, and to walk humbly with your God?" (Micah 6:8, NRSV)

5. Accountability: Lead with Honesty and Humility

Leaders welcome accountability, recognizing that leadership is a form of stewardship. Accountability ensures faithfulness to God and to the community. "So then, each of us will be accountable to God." (Romans 14:12, NRSV)

6. Responsibility: Stewardship of God's Call

Leadership is a sacred trust. Responsibility means caring for people, resources, and opportunities with diligence, knowing all belongs to God. "Who then is the faithful and wise, who has put in charge of his household, to give the others their allowance of food at the proper time? Blessed is that one whom his leader will find at work when he arrives." (Matthew 24:45–46, NRSV, adapted by author)

7. Gratitude: Lead with a Thankful Heart

A grateful leader sees every success as a blessing and every challenge as a lesson. Gratitude fosters humility, joy, and resilience. "Give thanks in all circumstances; for this is the will of God in Christ Jesus for you." (1 Thessalonians 5:18, NRSV)

8. Empowerment: Lift Others as God Lifts You

Leadership is not about control, but about empowering others to reach their full potential in their God-given gifts. A true leader makes disciples and builds community. "Therefore encourage one another and build up each other, as indeed you are doing." (1 Thessalonians 5:11, NRSV)

9. Celebration – Rejoice in God's Goodness

Celebration reminds leaders and communities to honor milestones, victories, and God's ongoing faithfulness. Celebrating together strengthens joy, unity, and hope. "Rejoice in the Lord always; again, I will say, Rejoice." (Philippians 4:4, NRSV)

"This is the day that the Lord has made; let us rejoice and be glad in it." (Psalm 118:24, NRSV)

10. Resilience and Perseverance – Endure in Faith

Leadership is not without trials. Resilience and perseverance enable leaders to remain steadfast, trusting in God during hardship and pressing forward with hope. "Let us not grow weary in doing what is right, for we will reap at harvest time, if we do not give up." (Galatians 6:9, NRSV)

"Blessed is anyone who endures temptation. Such a one has stood the test and will receive the crown of life that the Lord has promised to those who love him." (James 1:12, NRSV)

A Final Word for the Journey

To every Black woman leading today: You are not alone. Your journey, voice matters, rest and joy—matters. You may have many more rivers to cross. But remember—you come from a people who have always crossed waters and come out singing.

You are not sitting at the table. You are the whole house. You are not a problem waiting to be solved. You are a prophetess to be heard. You are a river. Keep crossing. Keep building. Keep believing.

— ***Rev. Dr. Christal L. Williams*** *is the Regional Minister of the Christian Church in Indiana. She is the first woman and African American to serve as the Regional Minister in Indiana and Tennessee.*

References

Hughes, L. (1994). *The Negro speaks of rivers.* In A. Rampersad and D. Roessel (Eds.), *The Collected Poems of Langston Hughes* (p. 23). Vintage Classics. (Original work published 1921)

New International Version. (2011). Holy Bible. Zondervan. (Revelation 22:1)

Pierce, Y.N. (2021). *In My Grandmother's House: Black Women, Faith and the Stories We Inherit.* Broadleaf Books.

Riley, C.A. (2022). *This Flesh: Spirituality, Liberation, and the Stories That Make Us.* Convergent Books. (Riley, 2022, p.172)

Riley, C.A. (2022, February 14). *This Flesh: A Conversation with Cole Arthur Riley.* Christians for Social Action. https://christiansforsocialaction.org/resource/this -her-flesh-a-conversation-with- Cole-Arthur-riley/

Thurman, H. (1971). *The Search for Common Ground: An Inquiry Into the Basis of Man's Experience of Community.* Harper & Row.

Truth, S. (1851). Ain't I a woman? Speech delivered at the Women's Convention, Akron, Ohio. In M. Robinson (Ed.), Anti-Slavery Bugle (June 21, 1851). Retrieved from https://www.nps.gov/articles/sojourner-truth.htm

An Encyclopedic Listing of African American Women Trailblazers

A Continuing Story in the Christian Church (Disciples of Christ)

Rev. Dr. Charisse L. Gillett

The Encyclopedia Britannica salesman did his best to convince my mom of the necessity of a complete set of encyclopedias. In his eagerness, he misread her intent. Mom had planned to purchase the books as an investment in her children's futures. And she did. In our home the volumes informed book reports and resolved sibling debates. We quickly learned the entries were an introduction to a subject. To learn more, we had to go to the library, ask questions, and dig deeper.

A Time for Honor: A Portrait of African American Clergywomen (2001), captures Dolores Carpenter's groundbreaking research on African American clergywomen pursing ordination. It remains a thoughtful, historically accurate account of the factors impacting the ordination and ministry opportunities for African American clergywomen across denominations. Women pursuing ordination and serving as associate pastors, ministers of Christian education, youth ministers, and—on rare occasions 30 years ago—seizing opportunities as senior pastors are trailblazers. They paved the way for a cadre of women serving as senior pastors of congregations in all contexts. These trailblazers endured Jim and Jane Crow and, in the modern era, confronted genderized and racialized perceptions of African American women that created barriers to leadership. They faced overt challenges and skepticism of their leadership and were judged more harshly and often than their counterparts. Nonetheless, they answered the call to share their gifts with the church. Their presence added new voices to the discourse and embodied the *soul* work of making God's kin-dom whole.

Dolores Carpenter, Cynthia Hale, and Robin Hedgegman in the 1980s are exemplars of these women. Representing today those who have served or are serving in the pulpits of historic African American churches are R. Janae

Pitts Murdock, pastor of Light of the World Christian Church; Crystal Chin, former interim pastor of Park Manor Christian Church; former and current pastors Judy Cummins and Tara Faith Williams of New Covenant Christian Church; Toni Colbert, the first woman to serve as the interim pastor of East Second Street Christian Church; and Dikiea Elery, the first woman called as the settled pastor of East Second Street. These women, along with those serving as associate pastors, Sandra Brown, and pastoral care clergy, Maudine Wordlaw, are exemplars of those who have inherited the mantel of leadership of African American congregations and who, by their presence, made it possible for others to become trailblazers.

Women who by their work in the Ministers' Wives Fellowship and their service alongside their spouses as First Ladies deserve honor. These women, recognizing their own contributions to the National Christian Missionary Convention (NCMC) and National Convocation (Disciples of Christ), at the 1988 National Convocation in Memphis commissioned a written history of their ministry for presentation at the 1990 Convocation. This booklet, *History of the Ministers' Wives,* written by Lucile A. Compton, is one the few historical records about the contribution of women during the early days of the National Convocation. Women who minister in Sunday school and Vacation Bible School programs are leaders. And of course, those called out by their communities of faith in the Black church tradition as Mothers of the Church are the moral and spiritual centers of congregations. They too are exemplars of female leadership. These women—all of them—have poured themselves into the foundation that gave birth to generations of women leaders.

The African American Women Trailblazers list is a continuation of the six volumes of *Disciples Who Made A Difference,* published by Disciples Home Missions, and an extension of the *History of the Minsters' Wives* booklet. These efforts to document the contributions of African American women to the Christian Church (Disciples of Christ) is an assertion of the community's agency. We are not invisible, and we will not be made invisible in history.

The list is an ongoing process to document African American Women Trailblazers in the Christian Church (Disciples of Christ). The list does not reflect all contributions made by African American women in the Christian Church. Frankly, this is an impossible task due to the lack of data on the contributions of women and women of color. Like the entries in the encyclopedias my mom purchased, this list is an introduction and establishes a baseline for future work. You are invited to dig deeper and join the process of documenting the soul work of African American women trailblazers in the Christian Church Disciples of Christ.

1. **Mary Alphin** in 1904, in conjunction with the Christian Women's Board of Missions (CWBM) of Texas, is credited with planting the seeds for what is now Jarvis Christian University.
2. **Lois Artis** was the first Black woman to lead a general unit of the Christian Church (Disciples of Christ). She served as president of the Church Finance Council and associate general minister and president of the Christian Church (Disciples of Christ) in the United States and Canada. Ms. Artis was the first African American woman nominated to serve in the role of general minister and president. Although the nomination was not successful, it signaled a shift in who should be considered to lead the church.
3. **Dietra Wise Baker** is an activist, educator, and pastor committed to racial justice. She served on the board of Disciples Homes Missions and received the Liberation Award from the National Convocation in 2016.
4. **Carnella Jameson Barnes** was the first African American president of the International Christian Women's Fellowship (ICWF) serving from 1974–1978. She worked as an organizer of women's societies with CWBM and subsequently, UCMS. She received the Liberation Award in 1990 from the National Convocation as an American Missionary Society Pioneer. (Black Disciples Who Made a Difference #1)
5. **Yvonne Barnes** was the first African American woman to serve as moderator of the Christian Church in North Carolina**.** She also served as a regional elder, gave leadership to supporting the offerings for Week of Compassion and CWF Blessing Box.
6. **A. Densie Bell** was the first African American woman to serve as regional minister of the Christian Church in Georgia (2014–2023). She is the first African American woman to hold the Donald and Lillian Nunnelly Endowed Chair in Pastoral Leadership at Lexington Theological Seminary. She is the recipient of the Dissertation of the Year Award and a Wabash Center Teaching Fellow.
7. **Katherine "Sister Katie" Blackburn** was the only African American Disciples missionary commissioned by the Foreign Christian Missionary Society to serve in the Congo. She served as a kindergarten teacher and evangelized at the Bolenge Mission from 1907 to 1910. (Disciples of Christ Historical Society).

8. **Candyce Black-Wells** served on the DHM Board (2009-2023) including serve as the chair of the Board. She also served on the Board for the Hope Partnership for Missional Transformation 2013-2019.

9. **India Bobadilla** served in three General Ministries of the Christian Church. She served as a Zone vice president for the Christian Church Foundation, an area director for the Pension Fund and as an executive in Global Ministries including service in the Office of Latin America.

10. **Sabetha Jenkins Booker** was the first woman to serve as president of Jarvis Christian College (1991–2008). At the time, Jenkins Booker was the first African American woman to be president of any higher education institution associated with the Christian Church (Disciples of Christ). In 2023, she received the prestigious Alexander Campbell Distinguished Service Award from Higher Education & Leadership Ministries of the Christian Church.

11. **Sarah Lue Bostick** (1896–1948) holds the distinction of being the first African American woman ordained in the Christian Church on April 24, 1892. She served many years as a field worker with the CWBM and as president of the Negro CWBM. The Christian Church Foundation honors her memory with a named fund. (Black Disciples Who Made a Difference #1)

12. **Rosa Brown Bracy** (1895–1960) was known as the Sojourner Truth of the NCMC. In 1938 she became the General Secretary of the NCMC. She was the first (1916-1938) Field Secretary of the CWBM. (Black Disciples Who Made a Difference #1)

13. **Billye P. Bridges** (1945–2012) served with the Division of Homeland Ministries, having nurtured churchwide educational programs with a focus on African Americans. In 2010, she received the National Convocation's Liberation Award. The National Convocation and the Division of Homeland Ministries honored her memory by naming its professional and ministerial educational programs at the Biennial Assembly of the National Convocation the Billye Bridges School of Faith and Life. (Black Disciples Who Made a Difference #4)

14. **Devetta Brown** was the first African American woman to serve as an associate regional minister of the Christian Church in South Carolina.

15. **Janis Brown** served an associate in the Office of Disciples Women with emphasis on the work of the National Convocation. She worked diligently to develop leadership training programs for women.

16. **Saundra Bryant** served as the executive director of the All Peoples Community Center for over 35 years. She served as a first vice moderator of the Christian Church, a trustee of the National Convocation Board, and as a member of the anti-racism committee of the Pacific Southwest Region. She is the recipient of the Martin Luther King Disciple of the Year award. (Black Disciples Who Made a Difference #5)
17. **L. Jackie Compton Bunch** is a lay woman committed to the Christian Women's Fellowship. She served as the board chair for the National Benevolent Association (NBA) and the Black Disciples Endowment Fund. In 2019, the NBA and the Christian Church Foundation established the Jackie Compton Bunch Fund.
18. **Nadine Burton** served in congregational and general church ministries, including service with Christian Church Extension Fund. She is the first African American woman to serve the Great River Region as the executive regional minister, traveling over 90,000 miles to serve churches and clergy (2015–2024). She is the vice president for the Great Lakes Zone of the Christian Church Foundation.
19. **LaTaunya M. Bynum** served as an associate regional minister for the Christian Church in Ohio. She chaired the search committee that called the first woman (Sharon E. Watkins) as the general minister and president of the Christian Church (Disciples of Christ). In 2014, she became the first African American and woman to serve as the regional minister of the Christian Church in Northern California-Nevada.
20. **Phyllis Byrd** began her career with Global Ministries in 1990 as a mission co-worker in Kenya with the Africa Council of Churches, and for ten years served as the director of Just Communications with the Organization of Africa Instituted Churches. (Global Ministries Celebrates Woman 2021)
21. **Brenda M. Cardwell** was the first African American woman to receive a Master of Divinity degree (1981) from Lexington Theological Seminary. She and Edward K. Fox Sr., co-authored Journey *Towards Wholeness: A History of Black Disciples in the Mission of the Christian Church.* She is the recipient of the Conductor Award from the Fellowship of Black Disciples Clergywomen.
22. **Dolores Carpenter,** scholar and pastor, served on the general board and administrative committee of the Christian Church. She served as the president of the National Convocation and in 2006 received the

organization's Liberation Award. In 2024 she received the Conductor Award from the Fellowship of Black Disciples Clergywomen. She is the General Editor of the *African American Heritage Hymnal.* (Black Disciples Who Made a Difference #3)

23. **Eliza Husser Cave** served as president of the South Carolina Convention (predecessor to the Regional Assembly). She served on the search committees for the Disciples general minister and president C. Williams Nichols and Richard L. Hamm. She received the Trailblazer Award for South Carolina Disciples Women in 2013. (Black Disciples Who Made a Difference #3)
24. **Daisy Chambers** (1936–2017) a layperson and founding member of Messiah Community Christian Church (Disciples of Christ). She served the Christian Church at the local, regional, and general levels on boards and committees. Her global service on behalf of Disciples women included mission trips to China, Zimbabwe, Haiti, and Brazil. (Black Disciples Who Made a Difference #6)
25. **Bessie E. Chandler** was named by NCMC leadership an Elementary Superintendent for her work with children and youth in Christian education. She helped to establish laboratory schools for teacher training in the 1950s. She is remembered for bridging the ministries of the National Christian Missionary Convention and the National Convocation.
26. **Crystal Chin** served as interim pastor of Park Manor Christian Church. She is the first woman to lead the church as pastor.
27. **Susie Cobb** was the first African American women ordained in the South Carolina region.
28. **Toni Colbert** served as interim pastor of East Second Street Christian Church during the COVID-19 global pandemic. She was the first woman to lead the church as pastor.
29. **Lucile A. Compton** established an endowed scholarship in 1988 with a gift of $500 so the women who had labored for the cause across the years would live on in history. She is the author of the booklet *History of the Ministers' Wives of the National Christian Missionary Convention and National Convocation of the Christian Church.* (Old Timers Grapevine Volume 16, Issue 2)
30. **Monique Crain-Spells** a theological educator and administrator served in senior leadership positions with Christian Theological Seminary and Brite Divinity School. She served as moderator of the Indiana region

and led the Fellowship of Black Clergywomen as president and is the vice president of Disciples Home Missions, giving fresh expression to historic documents from the Merger Agreement. Her Doctor of Ministry project, *The Power of Rituals to Nurture Embodied Worship* is under development as a book.

31. **Stephanie Buchannon Crowder** served on the general board and administrative committee. She was a Bible lecturer for the Biennial Session of the National Convocation and a contributing Lecturer to the Bible studies at the General Assembly. She is a Wabash Center for Teaching Fellow. She is the author of *When Momma Speakers* and a contributor to *True to Our Native Land: An African American New Testament Commentary.*
32. **Judy Cummings** a well-known community leader is pastor emerita of New Covenant Christian Church in Nashville. She was the first woman to serve the church as pastor.
33. **Ann E. Dickerson** (1936–1975) was elected vice moderator of the Christian Church at the San Antoino General Assembly. She served as a director of the Board of Higher Education, a trustee of the Pension Fund, and a member of the Tennessee Regional Board. A scholarship in her name was established for female Disciples students pursuing a PhD in religion. It is awarded annually by Higher Education & Leadership Ministries.
34. **Shannon Walker Dycus** was recognized by the Fellowship of Black Disciples Clergywomen for her leadership when she received the Conductor Award. In 2025, she was named interim president of Eastern Mennonite University, the first Black person to serve in that capacity. She is the author of *The Holy in the Night: Finding Freedom in a Season of Waiting.*
35. **Dikiea Elery** educator and community leader is the first woman to serve as the settled senior pastor of East Second Street Christian Church.
36. **Jane Elizabeth Martin Enix** (1906–1999) was an associate regional minister in the Indiana region from 1972 to 1975. She also served as the vice president for the National Convocation and was the first woman member of the National Interfaith Coalition on Aging. (Interview with L. Burnley, March 1990)
37. **Brenda Etheridge** is a past president of the International Disciples Women's Ministry and was a regional leader in the United States and Canada.

38. **Louise Evans** served in Disciples Home Missions with a focus on children's work, as well as Christian Women's Fellowship. At the time she was one of a handful of African Americans on staff in the General Office of the Christian Church (Disciples of Christ), serving in the Division of Homeland Ministries.

39. **Marilyn S. Fiddmont** is the first African American to serve as a vice president of the Christian Church Foundation's Southwest Zone. Through her 25-plus year ministry, she helped countless congregations, organizations, and individuals establish financial legacies that will serve their ministries in perpetuity.

40. **Melva Anderson Fields** (1928–2017) was a historian and advocate for women in ministry. She was passionate about the preservation of the history of Black Disciples and especially Black Disciples women. Along with her daughter, Rev. Sharon Fields, she co-authored, *In Other Words: Stories of African American Involvement in the Early Years of the Stone-Campbell Movement in Kentucky.* (Black Disciples Who Made a Difference #4)

41. **Sharon Fields,** educator and clergywoman, served as the first African American female moderator and first vice moderator of the Christian Church in Kentucky. She also served as the first vice president of the Kentucky Christian Missionary Convention. Along with her mother, she co-authored, *In Other Words: Stories of African American Involvement in the Early Years of the Stone-Campbell Movement.*

42. **Joyce Montgomery Foulkes** was the first African American woman to serve as the moderator of the Christian Church in Indiana, serving two terms. (Old Timers Grapevine)

43. **Deborah Garr** served on regional and national boards of the Christian Church and was well known as a leader in the women's ministry and music ministry throughout the church.

44. **Deetsy Blackburn Gary** was one of three women who in 1882 attended the Southern Christian Institute. She served for 16 years as an employee of the Christian Board of Publication.

45. **Charisse L. Gillett** is the first African American woman to serve as the moderator of the General Assembly of the Christian Church (2003–2005). In 2011, she became the first woman and African American to serve as president of Lexington Theological Seminary. In 2023, she was named a Woman of Distinction by the Association of Theological Schools Women in Leadership program.

46. **Yvonne Gilmore** is the first African American woman to serve in the senior leadership role for the National Convocation of the Christian Church as Interim Administrative Secretary 2020–2023.

47. **Mary Anne Glover** was the first African American woman to serve as a regional minister in the Christian Church (Disciples of Christ). She was called in 2008 as the transitional regional minister in the Northeastern region and was installed in 2012. She also served nine years as the associate regional pastor in the Christian Church in Ohio.

48. **Sandra Gourdet** began her career in Global Ministries in 1981, concluding her final years of service as the Africa Executive. In honor of her ministry and that of her spouse, the Gourdet Education Fund awards scholarships to support a student in Africa. In 1980 she received the Liberation Award from the National Convocation in 1980. (Global Ministries Celebrates Women 2021)

49. **Natalie S. Greene,** at the time of her election and service in 1979, was the youngest person elected to serve on the regional board of the Christian Church in Kentucky.

50. **Cynthia Hale** at the time of her service was the youngest person and first woman to serve as president of the National Convocation. She received the Liberation Award in 1984 and in 1985 she was the first woman nominated to become the administrative secretary of the National Convocation. Her nomination was not successful, and it was not until 2020 that a woman was called to the position. She is the founder of Ray of Hope Christian Church, serving 51 years as its senior pastor. She voices her story in *I'm a Piece of Work! Sisters Shaped by God* and is recognized as the voice of a new generation of preachers and leaders in Henry Louis Gates' *The Black Church.*

51. **Sandy Harvey,** church and business leader, served on local, regional, and general church boards of the Christian Church. She chaired the search committee for the regional minister of the newly drawn Living Waters Region, a tri-state region of Illinois, Wisconsin, and Michigan. She is the author of *The Inclusion Architecture Blueprint: A Seven Pillar Strategy for Transforming Workplace Culture.*

52. **Joan Bell Haynes,** is the first African American woman to serve as the executive regional minister of the Central Rocky Mountain Region and is the second African American and woman to serve as the regional minister of Georgia.

53. **Robin E. Hedgeman** has served as an associate regional minister in Ohio and president of the National Convocation. She has served as the senior pastor of Bethany Christian Church in Cleveland for twenty-eight years. Her call to action to the Christian Woman Fellowship led to the Cabinet selecting "Ending Racism" as the social action emphasis for the 1995–1998 quadrennium (p.186, *In The Fullness of Time*). She is an honoree of the National Council of Negro Women of Western Reserve.

54. **Claudia Highbaugh** in 1978 became the first African American woman ordained to the Christian Church (Disciples of Christ) after the 1968 Restructure and Merger. An educator, administrator, and committed churchwoman, she has served on numerous boards and committees in the church and institutions of higher education. (DDH Chicago Newsletter 2022)

55. **Dolores Highbaugh** (1927-2026) served as a vice moderator on the 1975–1977 moderator team of the General Assembly of the Christian Church (Disciples of Christ). She gave important leadership to Chicago Disciples Union, Christians Women's Fellowship, and her local church.

56. **Bernice Holmes** served in women's work and was a member of a team of staff people from NCMC that became a part of the United Christian Missionary Society in 1959.

57. **Anna Belle Jackson** served as director of Missionary Organizations for the NCMC from 1951–1969 and as the field staff worker for women's work from 1951–1960.

58. **Della January** served as president of the National Convocation from 1996–1998.

59. **Kathy Jeffries** was the first African American woman to serve as president of the Tennessee Christian Women's Fellowship. As vice president of the International Christian Women's Fellowship, she represented the General Assembly of the National Council of Churches and served on the Common Council of Church Women United USA. (Black Disciples Who Made a Difference #4)

60. **April G. Johnson** served as the minister and executive director of Reconciliation Ministries for the Christian Church (Disciples of Christ) from 2008–2025. She led the church in difficult conversations about restorative justice, race, and healing. In 2016, she received the Liberation Award from the National Convocation.

61. **Belva Brown Jordan** is the first African American woman to serve as the president/executive director of Disciples Seminary Foundation (2020–2023). She is the only moderator of the General Assembly of the Christian Church (Disciples of Christ) in the United States and Canada to serve two terms (2017–2019 and 2019–2023). She moderated the 2021 General Assembly which was held online due to the once in a lifetime global pandemic COVID-19. In 2023 she moderated the Louisville, Ky General Assembly.
62. **Julia Brown Karimu** served with general ministries of the Christian Church (DOC) for 44 years. She began her service in the Church in Society department of Disciples Home Missions. In 2012, she received the Liberation Award from the National Convocation. She is the first African American woman to serve as the President of the Division of Overseas Ministries and Co-Executive of Global Ministries (2011–2021). She is the recipient of an honorary Doctor of Divinity from Bethany College in Bethany, West Virginia.
63. **Mary Lou Kegler** served as the moderator of the regional board for the Christian Church in Greater Kansas City and as the second vice moderator for the General Assembly of the Christian Church (Disciples of Christ) from 2015–2017.
64. **Delesslyn Audra Kennebrew** is the former regional minister for Ministry Innovation for the Greater Kansas City Region (2018–2023). In 2023 she became the first African American woman to serve as the full-time permanent administrative secretary of the National Convocation of the Christian Church (Disciples of Christ). She is the author of *Step Out of the Boat: An Invitation to Walk on Water* and *The Power to be PERFECT: A Collection of Reflections on Spiritual Perfection.*
65. **Belinda King** is the first African American and woman to serve Disciples Church Extension Fund as president. She served as assistant treasurer for loan services and assistant vice president before assuming her role in 2021 as president. DCEF is one of three financial units of the Christian Church.
66. **Virzola Law,** an experienced church leader and pastor, is the first African American woman to serve as the Chair of the Board of Trustees for Brite Divinity School. She is a member of the Bethany Fellows Pastoral Leadership Initiative.
67. **Glenell M. Lee-Pruitt** became the 13th President of Jarvis Christian University, formerly Jarvis Christian College, in 2023. She is a recipient

of the United Negro College Fund Trailblazer Award. (Jarvis University website)

68. **Dara Cobb Lewis** was the first African American and woman to serve as the regional minister of the Christian Church in South Carolina and is a member of the Bethany Fellows Pastoral Leadership Initiative.

69. **Elsie "Dee" Long**, in a twenty-plus-year career, connected clergy, laity, and congregations to financial resources through Disciples Church Extension Fund and to valuable retirement resources from the Pension Fund. She is a well-known leader in the National Convocation, Churches of Christ-Disciples of Christ, and Disciples Women.

70. **Cherisna Jean Marie,** an educator and pastor, is the first African American woman to serve as the Dean of Disciples Divinity House at Vanderbilt School of Divinity.

71. **Ida Knight Melvin** served as the national president of Mission for the Church of Christ Disciples of Christ International.

72. **Valerie Melvin** in 2018 became the first woman and first African American to serve North Carolina as regional minister. She previously served as associate regional minister. In 2014, she received the Liberation Award. In 2014, Life Changing Ministries International Fellowship conferred upon her the title of Bishop.

73. **Eunice Miller** served from 1965–1968 as the National Christian Missionary Convention's director of the Department of Christian Women's Fellowship (CWF), working in the areas of social justice and leadership development. (*In the Fullness of Time*, p. 105)

74. **Regina Morton,** a laywoman from Tennessee, served as the moderator of the General Assembly of the Christian Church (Disciples of Christ) from 2011–2013. She presided over the 2013 General Assembly in Orlando, Florida.

75. **Lois Mothershed** served from 1961–1963 as director of development of the CWF. At the time she was the youngest woman appointed in the women's department. (*In The Fullness of Time,* p.104)

76. **R. Janae Pitts Murdock** is the first woman to serve as pastor of Light of the World Christian Church. She was also a member of the Board of the Disciples of Christ Historical Society.

77. **Janice Robinson Newborn** (1928–2019) served as CWF staff and executive for the Department of Church Women from 1983–1994. She received the Liberation Award in 2002 from the National Convoca-

tion. She is the originator of the Disciples Women's Woman-to-Woman (WTW) program. Since its inception, the WTW program has connected women across the globe in ministry and faith. (Obituary, 2020)

78. **Chesla Nickleson** served with the Office of Disciples Women with emphasis on the National Convocation.
79. **Teresa "Terri" Hord Owens** is the first African American woman to lead the Christian Church (Disciples of Christ) in the United States and Canada as general minister and president. At the time of her election in 2017, she was the first African American woman to lead a mainline denomination and serve as head of communion. She is the author of *Imagining a New World* and *Staying at the Table.*
80. **Patricia Parker** (1963–2015) served as president for the Mississippi Chrisitan Missionary Convention, on the regional board of the Great River Region, and on the planning committee for the Black Ministers Retreat. In 2002, she was installed as the first African American female pastor of a Disciples church in Mississippi. (Black Disciples Who Made a Difference #5)
81. **Patricia Ann Penelton** (1950–2025) a former president of the National Convocation had a lasting impact on the Convocation, at Central Christian Church in Kansas City and Centennial Christian Church in St. Louis, where she served as church moderator, vice moderator, deacon, usher, Christian Education chair, Worship co-chair, and choir member (Obituary 2025).
82. **Zellie Peoples** served as an International Christian Women's Fellowship advisory council member and was vice president of the organization in 1958. She served also as vice president of the NCMC from 1955–57 and 1959–65.
83. **Ann Pickett-Parker** an ordained clergy woman, has served as the president of the Mississippi Christian Missionary Convention for three terms.
84. **Syvoskia Bray Pope** a pastor and educator who served two terms as moderator of the Christian Church in Kentucky (2016–2018 and 2019–2021). She is the author of *12 Power Principles for Becoming the Woman God Called You to Be* and *Credit Champion: A Practical Guide to Leveraging Your Wealth and Increasing Your Purchasing Power.*
85. **Odatta Redd** served on the General Board and General Nominating Committee of the Christian Church (Disciples of Christ). She was vice-

president of the International Christian Women's Fellowship from 1986 to 1990. Redd has served in several capacities with the regional church in Virginia, as well as on the Virginia CWF Cabinet. (Black Disciples Who Made a Difference #2)

86. **May Reed** was a laywoman serving in CWF and on the board of directors for the National Convocation and Old Timers Grapevine. Known as the Poet Laureate of African American Disciples and the "keeper" of African American Disciples History, she received the Lifetime Service award from the Disciples Historical Society in 2024.

87. **Debra Reid** is the executive director for Disciples Women. She has served on the Tennessee Regional Board, National Convocation Board, International Women's Board and was selected as a 2023 Woman-to-Woman delegate to Japan and South Korea.

88. **Irie L. Session,** pastor and educator, served as the associate minister of the North Texas Area of the Christian Church in the Southwest. She is a founder and co-pastor of The Gathering: A Womanist Church, a church that centers the voices and strength of women for the flourishing of the whole church. She is the author of *Badass Women of the Bible.*

89. **Kamilah Hall Sharp,** pastor and educator, is a founder and co-pastor of the Gathering: A Womanist Church, a church that centers the voices of women. She is a recipient of the Ann E. Dickerson Scholarship and author of *Trauma and Survival in the Hebrew Bible.*

90. **Minnie Smith** served as vice moderator of the Christian Church during Richard Hamn's service as General Minister and President.

91. **Sheila P. Spencer** is the first African American woman to serve as the president of the Division of Homeland Ministries. She is the editor of the Oldtimers Grapevine and author of *The Gratitude Journal: Recharging Spirit, Reviving Body, and Renewing Soul.*

92. **Sybel A. Thomas** (1923–2011) served as the vice president of International Christian Fellowship from (1978–1982) and was a member of the first moderator team at the General Assembly of the newly restructured Christian Church (Disciples of Christ). She was also a former president of the National Convocation. She received the Liberation Award in 1998 from the National Convocation. (Black Disciples Who Made a Difference #4)

93. **Deborah Thompson** served as associate regional minister in Illinois-Wisconsin and went on to work at Disciples Church Extension with New Church Ministries.

94. **Maurica Thompson** served in the Office of Disciples Women, coordinating events for the Quadrennial Assembly for women.

95. **Laverne Thorpe** served as the vice president of International Disciples Women's Ministries. Her ministry brought attention and awareness to the training needed to address human trafficking on an international scale.

96. **Delores Turner** was the first African American woman to serve as the associate regional minister for the Christian Church (Disciples of Christ) in Indiana.

97. **Norma Ellington Twitty** was the first Black woman to hold an executive leadership position with the National Benevolent Association (NBA). From 1985–2007, she served as vice president of Program Planning and Evaluation. Her "yes" led to other Black women saying yes to NBA. She gives voice to her own story in the video *Voices of NBA: Black Women in Leadership.* She is the former President of the Old-timers Grapevine.

98. **Tanya J. Tyler** served as the board chair for the Christian Church Foundation and the Center for Faith and Giving. She is a two-term moderator of the CCIK (2008-2012) and is moderator elect for Christian Church in the Southwest region. An author, she has written for *Just Women and Chicken Soup for the Soul.* She and Charisse L. Gillett produced *Melodies of Fatih: An Advent Devotional for African American Churches and Families* and *Symbols of Fatih: A Lenten Devotional for African American Churches and Families.*

99. **Zola Walker** served as a vice moderator during Richard Hamn's term as General Minister and President.

100. **Rosa Page Welch** (1900–1994) was a teacher and a classically trained mezzo-soprano who had a promising concert career that she left to serve the church. Welch, born in Mississippi, is remembered as an Ambassador of Good Will. In 1952, she went on a trip singing to audiences in Africa, East Asia, Europe, and South America. Her prayers, *The Miracle of Communion* and *Joy Through Involvement* are published in the Chalice Hymnal. (Black Disciples Woman a Difference #2)

101. **Amelia Webb Walker,** a fourth-generation Disciple, is committed to gathering and sharing the history of African American Disciples through the Children of the Convention Project. The project chronicles family history and the history of African Americans in the NCMC and National Convocation.

102. **Margarette Wallick Webb** was a Quadrennial committee member in 1961 and vice president of the NCMC in 1960–61. At the time of her death in 1963, she was on the ICWF Advisory Council and the Committee on Brotherhood Restructure. (Children of the Convention Project).

103. **Marilyn Whittaker** was the first Black woman to serve as moderator for the Virginia Region. She dedicated herself to making sure every Virginia disciple found representation within the Administrative Council. She served as chair for Virginia's Anti Racism/Pro-Reconciliation Ministry.

104. **Christal L. Williams** served as an associate regional minister in Illinois-Wisconsin and as the regional minister in Tennessee. In 2024, she was called to serve as the regional minister of Indiana. She served as the president of the College of Regional Ministers and on the Boards of Christian Theological Seminary and Disciples Overseas Ministries. She is the author of the *Power of Asking* and *Beneath It All.*

105. **Marilyn F. Williams** served as the second vice moderator (2009–2011) of the Christian Church, president of the International Disciples Women Ministries (2014–2020), and president of the Disciples Women for National Convocation. She established the National Convocation Women's Endowment Fund. In North Carolina, Marilyn served as moderator and president of the NC CWF/DWM.

106. **Jamel Wright** became the 27th president of Eureka College and the first African American president in the school's history in 2017.

Reference

Brown, R.E. *The African American History*, p.34-35

Burnley, L A.Q. (2008). *The Cost of Unity: African American Agency and Education in the Christian Church (Disciples of Christ).* Mercer University Press, Macon, GA.

Burnley, L. A.Q. Interview with L. Burnley March 1990

Carpenter, D. (2001). *A Time For Honor: A Portrait of African American Clergywomen.* Chalice Press, St. Louis, MO.

Compton, Lucile A. *History of The Ministers' Wives: National Christian Missionary Convention and the National Convocation* (1990)

Craddock, F., Faw, M., and Heimer. *In the Fullness of Time: A History of Women in the Christian Church (Disciples of Christ),* p. 186. Chalice Press. St. Louis, MO (1999)

Disciples Who Made A Difference #1. Revised Edition (2004) www.discipleshomemissions.org
Disciples Who Made A Difference #2. www.discipleshomemissions.org
Disciples Who Made A Difference #3. www.discipleshomemissions.org
Disciples Who Made A Difference #4. www.discipleshomemissions.org
Disciples Who Made A Difference #5. www.discipleshomemissions.org
Disciples Who Made A Difference #6. www.discipleshomemissions.org
Global Ministries Celebrates Women 2021
The Link Published Quarterly for Alumni and Friends Volume 34 No.1 April 1995 Christian Theological Seminary, Indianapolis, IN
Oldtimers Grapevine Vol. 16 Issue 2 April-June

Continuing the Conversation

Questions for Reflection

Engaging the stories of these women is an invitation and opportunity to reflect upon one's own leadership journey. Never forget that it is in conversation with God that transformation and growth begins. We invite you to consider these questions as part of your journey towards transformation and flourishing.

1. How has your origin story informed your ministry? Leadership?
2. What aspects of the women's narrative resonate with your journey?
3. In what ways have you been as source of support and/or discomfort for African American women in leadership?
4. How do you attend to your leadership growth and development?
5. Who are your personal trailblazers?
6. How do you honor the ministry of these trailblazers?
7. What legacy would you like to leave to the next generation of leaders?
8. Are you flourishing? Why? Why not?
9. What three steps can you take towards flourishing?
10. What is your Soul Story?

The invitation my sisters is to learn, to grow, and to flourish in your own skin.

The African American Women Trailblazers

The African American Women Trailblazers list at the conclusion of this book documents the contributions to the Christian Church (Disciples of Christ) of more than 100 African American women. With assistance from the Disciples of Christ Historical Society, Higher Education & Leadership Ministries, and the families of some of these woman, here are some of the faces to accompany the names of those whose work and ministry has opened doors for future African American women leaders in the church.

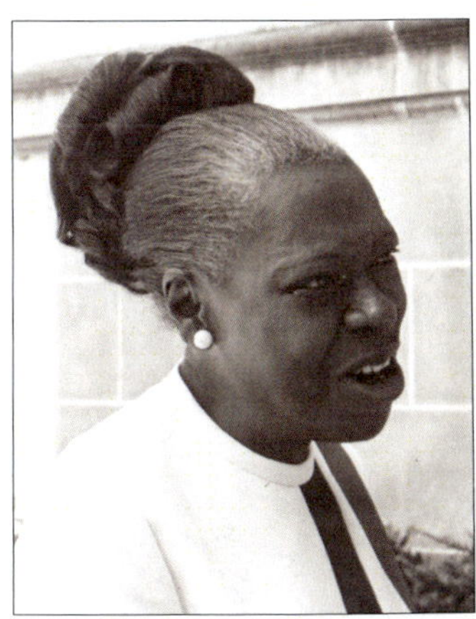

Carnella Jameson Barnes

Sebetha Jenkins Booker

A. Denise Bell

Sarah Lue Bostick

Rosa Brown Bracy

Nadine Burton

Billye P. Bridges

LaTaunya M. Bynum

Saundra Bryant

Phyllis Byrd

Dolores Carpenter

Dara Cobb-Lewis

Eliza Husser Cave

Monique Crain Spells

Daisy Chambers

Stephanie Buckhannon Crowder

Ann E. Dickerson

Sharon Fields

Marilyn Fiddmont

Charisse L. Gillett

Melvia Anderson Fields

Cynthia Hale

Joan Bell-Haynes

Claudia Highbaugh

Robin Hedgeman

Terri Hord Owens

Dolores Highbaugh

Kathy Jeffries

Belva Brown Jordan

Janice R. Newborn

Delesslyn A. Kennebrew

Patricia Parker

Valerie Melvin

Ann Pickett-Parker

May Reed

Norma Ellington Twitty

Sheila P. Spencer

Rosa Page Welch

Sybel A. Thomas

Christal L. Williams